THE ART OF LION DANCE

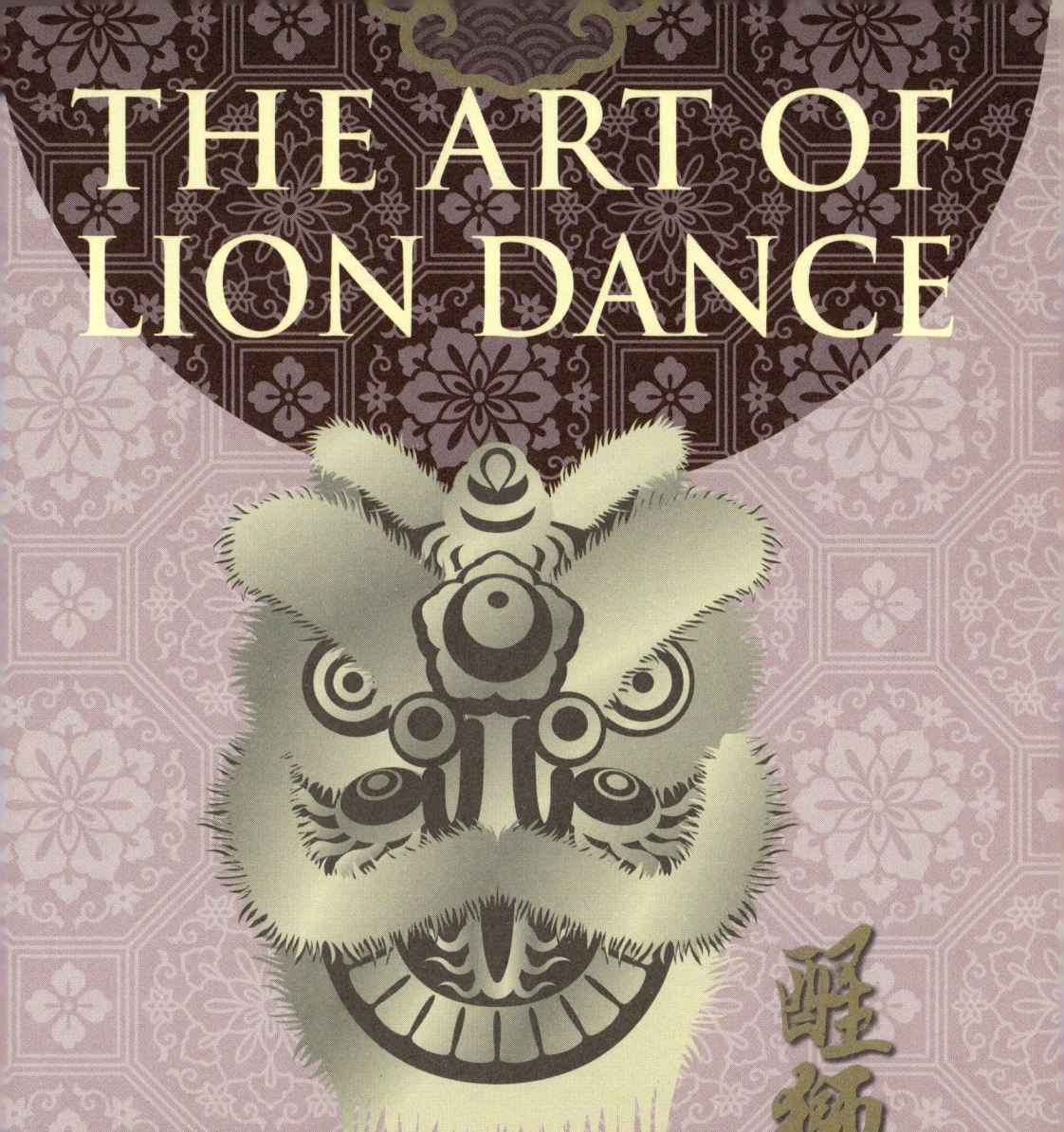

醒獅

Joey Yap's
The Art of Lion Dance

All intellectual property rights including copyright in relation to this book belong to Joey Yap Research Group Sdn. Bhd.

No part of this book may be copied, used, subsumed, or exploited in fact, field of thought or general idea, by any other authors or persons, or be stored in a retrieval system, transmitted or reproduced in any way, including but not limited to digital copying and printing in any form whatsoever worldwide without the prior agreement and written permission of the copyright owner. Permission to use the content of this book or any part thereof must be obtained from the copyright owner. For more details, please contact:

JOEY YAP RESEARCH GROUP SDN BHD (944330-D)
19-3, The Boulevard, Mid Valley City,
59200 Kuala Lumpur, Malaysia.
Tel   : +603-2284 8080
Fax   : +603-2284 1218
Email   : info@masteryacademy.com
Website : www.masteryacademy.com

Copyright © 2016 by Joey Yap Research Group Sdn. Bhd.
All rights reserved.
First Edition December 2016

DISCLAIMER:

The author, copyright owner, and the publishers respectively have made their best efforts to produce this high quality, informative and helpful book. They have verified the technical accuracy of the information and contents of this book. However, the information contained in this book cannot replace or substitute for the services of trained professionals in any field, including, but not limited to, mental, financial, medical, psychological, or legal fields. They do not offer any professional, personal, medical, financial or legal advice and none of the information contained in the book should be confused as such advice. Any information pertaining to the events, occurrences, dates and other details relating to the person or persons, dead or alive, and to the companies have been verified to the best of their abilities based on information obtained or extracted from various websites, newspaper clippings and other public media. However, they make no representation or warranties of any kind with regard to the contents of this book and accept no liability of any kind for any losses or damages caused or alleged to be caused directly or indirectly from using the information contained herein.

INDEX

Preface   4

Chapter One: 9
Introduction

Chapter Two: 51
The Lion and The Craft

Chapter Three: 105
The Art of Lion Dance

Chapter Four: 151
Lion Dance Traditions and Practices

Chapter Five: 197
Qi Men Methodologies in Lion Dance

Chapter Six: 243
Hiring a Troupe for Qi Men Lion Dance

Preface

The Lion Dance is an internationally recognised symbol of Chinese culture. As a young boy, the Lion Dance made an indelible impression on me. My parents would take my siblings and I to watch Lion Dance performances during Chinese New Year. Back then, they were more than just entertaining shows – they were a competitive spectacle! If two dance troupes met they would engage in a fierce showdown of mesmerizing movement, colour and drums!

Because I am a Feng Shui practitioner and scholar of Chinese metaphysics, people often assume that I am clued up on all aspects of Chinese culture, including the Lion Dance. Truth be told, it was only recently that I decided to study its origins and meaning. My research taught me a lot about Chinese culture as a whole. I began to share my findings with some of my students and clients, and it wasn't long before some of them suggested I write a book on the matter.

Researching the Lion Dance, I found that it has strong ties to Qi Men Dun Jia: an aspect of metaphysics that I am especially interested in. This connection intensified my interest in the dance, spurring me to travel to China, Hong Kong and Taiwan to conduct further research. This book is the fruit of my labours.

The ritualistic and metaphysical roots of the Lion Dance are easy to overlook. Perhaps this is because these aspects have been overshadowed by the sheer spectacle and fun of the modern Lion Dance.

Since ancient times, the lion has been seen as a symbol of power, wisdom, longevity and good fortune. Lions are a staple of Chinese folklore, literature and art. In the context of dance, the lion can usher in and activate favourable energy and dispel negativity. In its early incarnations, the Lion Dance was used to invigorate imperial soldiers before they marched into battle. It was also used in civilian ceremonies to help ward off evil.

Today, the Lion Dance is still used in ceremonies and festivities to help usher in positive energy, or Qi – the circulating life force at the heart of Chinese metaphysics. Feng Shui practitioners endeavour to increase one's exposure to positive Qi in a space. In much the same way, one can use a Lion Dance in accordance with metaphysical directions and principles to help usher Qi into their home or business. Choosing the right date and direction for such a Lion Dance is important, a concept also found in Qi Men Dun Jia.

Qi Men Dun Jia is a system used to plot the flow of Qi across time and space. It describes the movement of energy in different directions with great accuracy. With an understanding of Qi Men, a practitioner can identify the time and place where positive Qi will be present. By scheduling an activity with such foreknowledge, one can take advantage of the prevailing positive energy. The Lion Dance ties into Qi Men because it is known that human activity can activate positive Qi. A Lion Dance troupe's performance can amplify Qi; with the right footwork and direction of movement, performers can help bring their audience good fortune.

In this book, you can expect to learn all about the meaning behind the choreography, tools, music, design, blocking, timing and direction that make up a successful Lion Dance. The next time you watch a Lion Dance, I promise you will do so with more appreciation than ever before. Researching this subject has given me a newfound appreciation of why performance artists do what they do. As your knowledge of the Lion Dance grows, you can request one to help further your own personal and professional fortune.

I hope you enjoy reading about this fascinating spectacle and at the very least you'll have a lot to tell your friends and family during the festive season when you hear the gong beats!

Warmest Regards,

Dato' Joey Yap
New York, October 2016

Connect with us:

www.joeyyap.com   JOEYYAP TV   www.joeyyap.tv

@DatoJoeyYap   @DJoeyYap   @JoeyYap

Academy website:
www.masteryacademy.com | jya.masteryacademy.com | www.baziprofiling.com

BONUS CONTENT
FREE DOWNLOAD

Exclusive content available for download with your purchase of the The Art of Lion Dance book.

Gain immediate access to Bonus video from Dato' Joey Yap by claiming your FREE ONLINE ACCESS now at:

www.masteryacademy.com/bookbonus2017

ALD17BC3

Chapter 1
Introduction

吉時吉方

There is nothing more quintessentially Chinese than the Lion Dance. There are few people in the world who can't conjure up an internal image of the ornate and colourful lions held aloft by the athleticism of the dancers. The open mouth and hypnotic eyes of the 'Lion'. The rhythmic drums and the cymbals. The sheer spectacle and excitement of the event. The undulating beast takes on a life, in our imaginations, far beyond the sum of its parts, the theatre of the dance draws us in and we leave our disbelief behind, for a few shorts moments, to become part of a different time and place.

All over the world, from America to Europe, from Australia to Africa to Polynesia, you don't have to be an expert on Chinese culture to instantly recognise this fascinating element of Chinese tradition. The Lion Dance represents an all pervasive image of a culture and heritage that has spread all over the world, thanks to the tenacious and resilient nature of the Chinese people whose diaspora have come to call a multitude of different nations their home.

醒獅

The Lion Dance is an ancient Chinese art form that today is performed worldwide

In spite of this, how many people, who have stood by and watched the show, whether in person or on their television screens, truly understands the tremendously long history, and the real significance of the Lion Dance to Chinese culture? The very fact that it has become so familiar to so many, alone, stands as testament to the importance of the Lion Dance in the hearts of the Chinese people. Wherever they have traveled, they have taken this very special part of their homeland and of their traditions with them. As the years have passed, their passion for the Lion Dance has remained strong and it is as relevant, as valued and as vital now as it ever was.

The Art of Lion Dance

The Lion Dance has existed for more than a thousand years and it is so much more than just a display of artistry and gymnastics. In addition to music, song and movement, the Lion Dance is believed to be a kind of space and energy activation ritual. More than just court entertainment, it is the merging of metaphysics and art, beauty and science.

The Lion Dance forms a traditional part of special occasions. The dance will always be performed at significant festivals, like Chinese New Year, but it can also be a component of weddings, celebrations, officiation events and even funerals. The powerful, martial arts based, movements of the dancers play a very important role in these events, it is their responsibility to frighten away evil spirits

Northern Lion (Bei Shi 北獅)

and open the way for more positive energy and good fortune. Of course the basis of the metaphysical element is, in truth, far more complex than this basic explanation reveals, as is the history of the involvement of martial arts in the dance.

Though many regional forms of the Lion Dance exist, the most famous are the Northern Lion (*Bei Shi* 北獅) and the Southern Lion (*Nan Shi* 南獅). The Northern Lion (*Bei Shi* 北獅) is recognisable as it is a dance performed between a pair of lions, one male and one female, or even a family of lions, while the Southern Lion (*Nan Shi* 南獅), by far the most famous of the two, certainly on a global stage, usually involves a single lion.

Southern Lion (Nan Shi 南獅)

The involvement of martial arts in the Lion Dance performance developed and become more pronounced as a result of the Cultural Revolution. During this rather turbulent and complex time in Chinese History, the Maoist movement sought to transform elements of Chinese culture to bring it more in line with Maoist doctrine. One of the elements that they sought to control were the Martial Arts Schools. In an attempt to protect their independent lineages, the various Martial Arts schools began to incorporate an array of their most famous moves into the Lion Dance.

These attempts by the Martial Arts Schools to preserve their lineages through dance had an incredible influence on the art form as a whole, and not only lead the Lion Dance into taking on a very recognisably martial flavour, but also recreated the Lion Dance as a competitive sport. The downside to this rebirth was that the Lion Dance, for a time, became associated with radical and subversive elements in society which deepened an already negative connection with the triads that had plagued the dance since the Qing Dynasty.

The modern Lion Dance is more closely linked to Chinese martial arts than it is to Chinese Metaphysics nowadays.

This unsavoury reputation was not salvaged until the later half of the twentieth century, largely thanks to Hong Kong Cinema. It was then that the Lion Dance was portrayed, not as something subversive but as a means of creating unity, a symbol of brotherhood and honour. The Shaw Brothers Studio did a great deal to revamp the image of the Lion Dance when it released such movie classics as *Lion vs Lion* in 1991, *Kids from Shaolin* in 1984 and *Once Upon a Time in China* in 1991.

Today, the Lion Dance is an increasingly complex and challenging art form. There are championships that take place all over the world on a yearly basis. Anywhere where there is a large Chinese population, like Malaysia, Singapore, Taiwan and Hong Kong, there is a Lion Dance competition that tests the mettle of its performers. The elaborate choreography now no longer involves just acrobatics, but also daring stunts involving stilts and elevated platforms.

While this competitive edge has helped the Lion Dance to evolve as an art form, and has made it so tremendously exciting as a spectacle, it has also acted to overshadow the metaphysical aspects of the dance that were once considered to be so very important. While most dancers and spectators may know that the dance is designed to ward off bad luck or to act as a blessing or good luck charm at major events, few will know about the true complexities of the spiritual aspects of the dance.

To those of us with an interest in metaphysics, it cannot be anything but a disappointment that something so fascinating, and so potentially life changing, could have been so easily forgotten. It is my hope, that throughout these pages, we will be able to redress the balance and restore the Lion Dance to its full splendour as an art form, a connecting force between disparate Chinese populations, a beautiful link to China's fascinating and colourful past and cultural legacy and a powerful spiritual and metaphysical force to be reckoned with.

History and Origins

The Lion Dance dates back many, many centuries to a time when China, as we know it, was first formed after the unification of rival tribes and principalities. A union that was by no means a stable one. The history of the dance is therefore intimately tied to politics, society and the evolution of Chinese culture. It is impossible to study the history of the dance without looking at the history of China and working to understand the role that the Lion Dance, and indeed dance and ritual as a whole, have played in Chinese mythology and symbolism from the very birth of Chinese civilisation.

Qi is the circulating life force that forms the basis of many Chinese Metaphysics concepts

Although the Xia Dynasty 夏朝 (2070 – 1600 B.C.) is traditionally understood to have been the very first of the Chinese dynasties, having been described in various ancient texts, there is no archeological evidence of its existence. Many historians have, therefore, come to believe that this dynasty was the stuff of legend, passed down by word of mouth from one generation to the next before finally been committed to the written word thousands of years after the original tales of its exploits were first circulated. Our study into the history of dance and ritual in Chinese culture will therefore begin with the Shang Dynasty.

The Shang Dynasty 商朝 (1046 – 256 B.C.) is the first of the Chinese dynasties the existence of which can be corroborated by archeological evidence. The rulers of the Shang Dynasty claimed to have been descended from the gods and that their rule was given legitimacy by the mandate of Heaven. Each of the emperors that ruled over this great dynasty was understood by their subjects to be the earthly counterpart to the Jade Emperor who ruled over the heavens and, indeed, to be the Son of Heaven here on earth.

The role of dance in these early dynasties was not simply a matter of courtly entertainment. The dances that were performed at court carried great symbolism as shows of power, and as rituals to connect the emperor to the heavens in order that he may ask the gods to bring to bear the full force of their heavenly powers in support of his earthly reign.

It was not, however, just the emperor who could make use of dance as a display of power and as a means to bring positive energy to bear upon his endeavours. *Di Xin* 帝辛, the last of the emperors of the Shang was overthrown by the Zhou Dynasty 周朝 (1046 – 256 B.C.), supported by other rebellious factions within the country in the year 1046 B.C. It is said that the armies of the Zhou sang and danced as they marched upon the capital following their historic victory. As the Zhou worked to unite a number of different factions

Pillars of Asoka found in Bodh Gaya, India. Images of lions such as these may have first made its appearance in China via the spread of Buddhism.

and tribes under their rule, it was they who first started to collate the many different songs, dances and rituals that were performed throughout the nation. In this way, they sought to create a sense of unity and to win the ongoing loyalty of their vassals. They would use these dances and rituals in important ceremonies and in celebrations at court.

At this time, the dances they used fell roughly into two categories: martial and civil. The martial dances often made use of uniforms, tails and feather related not just to military exploits but also to hunting and other traditionally masculine pursuits. These martial dances were very much perceived as a display of power and could be used in celebration of military exploits as well as a means of intimidation. Civil dances obviously had a less aggressive flavour.

Han Dynasty 漢朝 (206 B.C. – 220 A.D.)

One of the great mysteries of the Lion Dance is how an animal that is not native to China came to be the basis of a dance that has become so central to Chinese culture and tradition. The answer may be found in the ways in which the emperors of the Han Dynasty interacted with foreign powers and with the foreign influences that entered the country as a result of increasing trade. The lion was certainly introduced to China from without and even the Lion Dance itself may have found its origins elsewhere. Indeed there are variations on the theme of a Lion Dance that exist independently of their famous Chinese counterparts: the Indonesian Barong dance which represents the eternal struggle of good and evil being a case in point.

There are various theories about how the lion came to be known and recognised in China as well as why it may have become to be such an important symbol of power. One of the most popular theories is that the lion, and possibly even the Lion Dance, were introduced to China from India and Persia as trade links were created on the Silk Road. Ethnomusicologist Laurence Pickens has indeed theorised that the Chinese word for lion, "*Shi* 獅", may have been derived from the Persian word for Lion which is "šer".

There is a fair amount of evidence to support this contention. The term "*Shi Zi* 獅子" first appeared in the Chinese lexicon during the Han Dynasty, a time in which closer diplomatic ties and trade links to both India and Persia were being fostered. It is understood that emissaries from Central Asia presented lions to the Chinese court as gifts and that, equally, emissaries and diplomats sent out to the west to create trade links and to expand Chinese influence returned to the country with a host of exotic animals, including peacocks and lions.

The first recorded appearance of a lion in China was during the reign of Emperor *Wu* 武帝 of the Han. Emperor *Wu* reigned from 141-87 B.C. and is known to have sent imperial envoy *Zhang Qian* 張騫 on a diplomatic mission to the West, hoping to expand his influence and to win alliances with the *Yuezhi* 大月氏 and the *Xiongnu* 匈奴. When he returned with a wealth of discovery and information to share, he also brought a lion with him.

During this exciting time in Chinese history, a wealth of new information, new merchandise and new experiences would have flooded the country. The court would have become a busy place hosting diplomatic events and entertaining and being entertained by foreign envoys. One of the entertainments that may have came in from beyond Han borders lion tamers who would perform displays that must have been an incredible spectacle to behold. Could these have been the origin of the Lion Dance as we know it today?

Alternatively, it is possible that the birth of the Lion Dance may have had a more spiritual origin. It is generally believed that Buddhism reached China in the first century A.D. Emperor *Ashoka* was one of the greatest emperors in Indian History and reigned over almost the entire Indian sub-continent from 268-232 B.C. After witnessing the destruction from the Kalinga war, he converted to Buddhism and dedicated the end of his reign to propagating the philosophy among his people. This was the first wide expansion of Buddhism as a religion and popular philosophy, the lion was often regarded as the emblem of Emperor *Ashoka* whose influence on the faith must still have been keenly felt when it first reached the notice of the Chinese two centuries later.

Though it is tempting to look at these theories and believe that the Lion Dance may have had one common origin, it is also entirely possible that different regional variations of the dance evolved separately, influenced by a host of cultural developments. It is possible, even likely, that the earliest forms of what was to become the Lion Dance were influenced by the shamanistic rituals that formed the basis of early Chinese religious life and that they would have been performed in a host of different formats all over the country. As Chinese culture changed and evolved, so the Lion Dance changed and evolved, incorporating new elements and moving in different directions.

As Buddhism overtook Shamanism as a dominant religious philosophy, the practices of the old Shamans would have been increasingly regarded as uncivilised or even barbaric. As is often the case when a new religion enters a country, elements of the ancient traditions would have been adopted and sanitised to make them more suitable to new perspectives. As Buddhism gained in popularity, the ancient dances will have taken on elements of Buddhist philosophy and incorporated Buddhist tales and morality into their structures so the Lion Dance as we have come to now could well have been a Buddhist evolution of early shamanic practices.

Equally, during the Han Dynasty, dances and other spectacles that were performed at court for the entertainment of the emperor would have been managed by government officials. These performances would have included a host of different influences from every corner of the empire, the folk songs and dances of minority groups would have been among them. With the status granted by royal approval, these art forms would likewise have changed and evolved, becoming more refined and developing increasingly militaristic overtones. The new versions of these dances would in their turn have gone on to influence the evolution of the performances enjoyed by the general population.

During the Wei Dynasty, Lion Dances were described to have been performed alongside parades held in conjunction with the Buddha's birthday celebrations, possibly in Buddhist temples such as this one found in Luoyang, Henan.

Northern Wei Dynasty 北魏 (386 – 534 A.D.)

There are texts available from the time that indicate that by the Northern Wei, lions and early versions of the Lion Dance were definitely strongly associated with Buddhism.

On the 4th day of the 4th Lunar month a celebration would be held in honour of the Buddha's birthday. During this celebration, a statue of the Buddha would be escorted out of the temple on a parade and that lions were an important part of this procession. Texts suggest that dancers imitating lions would perform as part of the procession escorting the statue to frighten away evil spirits. Similar dances would have been incorporated into performances in celebration of the solstices and particularly of the Lunar New Year.

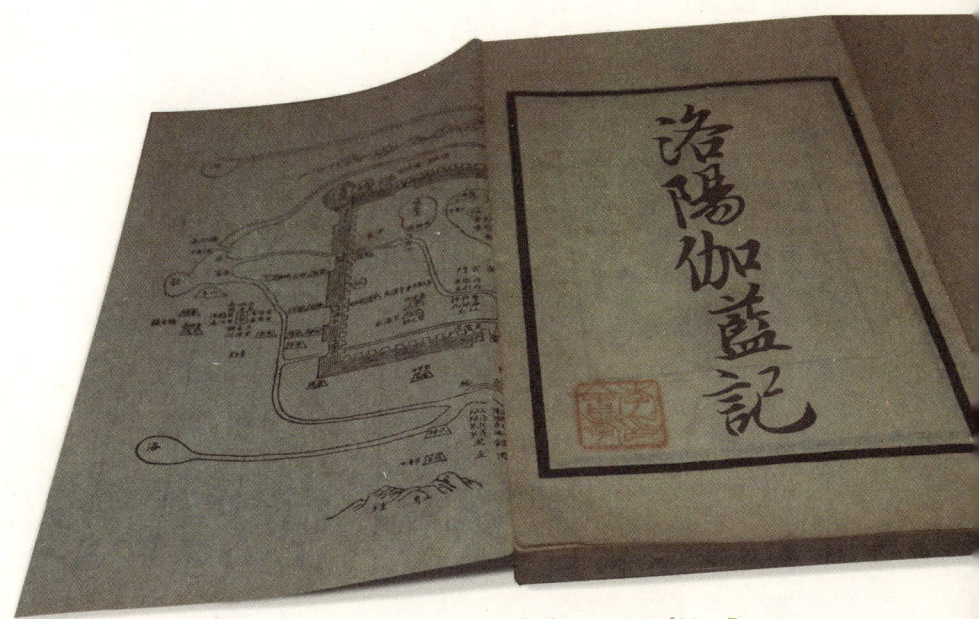

An early description of Lion Dances being used in conjunction with Buddhist celebrations was found in the Northern Wei text, Description of Buddhist Temples in Luoyang (Luo Yang Qie Lan Ji 洛陽伽藍記).

Jin Dynasty 晋朝 (265 – 420 A.D.)

晋 Records of the Jin Dynasty make clear mention of dance performances that featured elaborate lion costumes. There are two theories on the origins and influences behind the dance style that was used. Some of the evidence suggests that it was derived from the Masked Play (*Jia Min Xi* 假面戲) of the Western Liang, however, it is also possible that it evolved as a stylised version of the imperial troop's fighting style.

The "Masked Play", another Chinese performance that greatly influenced the Lion Dance.

The Art of Lion Dance

Tang Dynasty 唐朝 (618 – 907 A.D.)

The Lion Dance, really came into its own during the Tang Dynasty. It is believed that this dynasty saw the evolution of the Northern and Southern versions of the Lion Dance that we recognise today. It was also during the Tang Dynasty that the concept of the Lion Dance was exported to Japan where it is known as Shishimai.

The Lion Dance was considered to be one of the greatest performances to be staged at the imperial palace and it was a tremendous spectacle indeed. Known as the Great Peace Music (*Tai Ping Yue* 太平樂) or the Lion Dance of the Five Directions (*Wu Fang Shi Zi Wu* 五方師子舞), it featured five large lions, each one a different colour and each one reflecting a different mood, being manipulated on ropes each by two individuals. Each lion was said to be over three metres tall and each was accompanied by twelve 'lion boys' who would tease them with red whisks. Along side of the dancers would be a group of 140 singers and musicians.

According to the poet *Bai Juyi* 白居易, who described the Lion Dance in his book of poetry, Xi *Liang Ji* 西涼伎, the performers wore large lion masks made out of wood with golden eyes and silver teeth and that they wore a pelt made out of fur.

It appears therefore, that this particular version of the Lion Dance was definitely known to have been an import and it is known that this version came to be exceedingly influential. In addition to his descriptions of the dancers' costumes, *Bai Juyi* also mentions that the dance was very popular with the military and in addition to being performed at the palace, it was frequently performed by soldiers in their camps and barracks. As the troops were deployed to different locations throughout the empire, they would have taken these performances with them, exposing more and more of the population to this spectacular art form.

The Lion Dance that was performed in the Tang court was described in Xi Liang Ji 西涼伎 and looked similar to this illustration.

Northern Song Dynasty 北宋 (960 – 1127 A.D.)

Although the Lion Dance had previously been recognised as having been popular with the military and having a certain martial or military style to its performances, it was not until the Northern Song that the dance become connected explicitly with the martial arts. This lead to the evolution of a very new style of Lion Dance. At the same time, the Lion Dance was increasing in popularity among the common people of China which lead to the dividing of the dance into very obvious civilian and martial styles.

According to tradition, a martial arts master by the name of *Yang Xian Qiang* 楊顯槍 lived in the Western part of the city of *Lin Hai* 臨海市 in an area known as *Huang Sha Yang* 黃沙洋. He took the Lion Dance and moulded it into something completely new. In addition to incorporating a range of high leaps, jumps, balances and kicks as incorporated from the martial style that he taught, he also completely revolutionised the costume. He is credited with changing the old wooden masks and headdresses into papier-mache ones that were lighter and easier to carry, long strands of hemp were added to the body of the lion to create the impression of a shaggy coat, but this hemp was also dyed in bright colours, making the new lions multicoloured. This new version of the Lion Dance was known as the *Huang Sha Lion* 黃沙獅子 and is regarded to have been the starting point of the athletic and competitive Lion Dance that is still performed today

Among the general population, civilians however, were making the dance their own. They were not trained in the martial arts and did not have the skills necessary to manage the complex acrobatics, their versions were more playful involving tumbling, rolling over and playing with balls. When the Laughing or Big-Headed Buddha was added to these performances they were even known to take on something of a comedic overtone.

A typical Huang Sha Lion's 黃沙獅子 *appearance*

Ming Dynasty 明朝 (1368 – 1644 A.D.)

During the Ming Dynasty, the Lion Dance look on yet another new element to its performance. It was during the Ming Dynasty that Neo-Confucianism was born and adopted as the central philosophy of the state for all legal and bureaucratic purposes. Neo-Confucianism combined elements of Daoism, Confucianism and Buddhism into a new synthesis. The result of this was that the Lion Dance, which had previously been heavily influenced by Buddhism, came to take on a variety of Daoist influences such as the Four Realms, the Five Elements and the Eight Directions.

At this stage Daoist adepts began to recreate the dance as ritual rather than simply performance. They devised specific steps that were designed to activate energy and to communicate with the heavens. It is believed that this is also the time when Daoist Metaphysics systems such as Qi Men Dun Jia was incorporated into the dance routine. Elements such as Time, Space, Event and Spirit was connected with Human Energy through the unification of the physical body, mind, soul and rhythm.

At the same time, the costume underwent another new innovation. Where the lion head had been constructed around a middle column, they now began to be constructed around an arched instead. The effect of this was twofold, the head took on a more rounded and realistic shape and at the same time, the dancers were able to develop a better range of movement as the new design was easier to manipulate.

Qing Dynasty 清朝 (1644 – 1912 A.D.)

The Qing Dynasty was a time of famine, hardship and revolutionary fervour which saw the Lion Dance first being used as a tool of dissent and also saw the Lion Dance first being performed by the Chinese diaspora as they spread out to all four corners of the globe. During the early part of the Qing Dynasty an effort was underway to restore the former Ming Dynasty to power. Loyalists would use the Lion Dance as a cover for exchanges of money and information.

It is believed that when the Lion Dance first began to be used as a cover for the revolutionary hopefuls, the lead dancer would literally cry out "*Cai Qing* 踩清", 'Depose the Qing' in order to indicate the dancer's affiliations to the surrounding crowds. Obviously, this was not a very subtle approach and any Qing sympathiser in the crowd would quickly become aware of their intentions. The secret to a more delicate exchange of information was to be found in the format of the dance itself and in the similarity of the words "*Qing* 清", referring to the Qing Dynasty, and "*Qing* 青", which is the Chinese word for green.

During the Lion Dance, it is a customary for the lion to eat a lettuce as part of the dance routine. Instead of shouting out "*Cai Qing* 踩清" 'Depose the Qing', the dancers therefore came to shout out *Cai Qing* 採青 "Pluck the Greens". Any information or money that was to change hands would then be hidden inside of the lettuce. To this day, lion dancers will still call out *Cai Qing* 採青 when it comes time to consume the symbolic greens.

Towards the end of the Qing Empire, famine and civil unrest saw the first waves of Chinese immigrants departing their homeland in search of a better life on foreign shores. These early adventurers, bravely seeking to start afresh on foreign soil, travelled all over the world but a large majority settled in parts of South East Asia and the Americas. They brought their culture and customs with them, including the Lion Dance. Removed from the influence of the mother nation, these disparate populations were soon to develop their own unique regional styles.

It is also important to note that the legendary folk hero Master *Huang Fei Hong* 黃飛鴻 lived during the Qing Dynasty. In addition to his many accomplishments as a physician and as a Martial Artist, Huang Fei Hong was also a known proponent of the Lion Dance. He is believed to have popularised the Southern Lion Dance in *Foshan* 佛山, a city located in central Guangdong Province in southeastern China. In his approach to the dance, he incorporated both martial arts and local folk traditions creating the Awakened Lion on High Poles (*Gao Zhuang Xing Shi* 高樁醒獅) version of the dance, in which the dancers would perform complicated stunts on high poles or stilts.

Cai Qing 採青 Pluck the Greens

The Art of Lion Dance

Modern Era

The persecution of martial artists by the Red Guards had a significant impact on the evolution of the Lion Dance in the modern era. While some sought to preserve their martial arts in the movements of the dance, others were forced to flee China altogether, taking the Lion Dance and their own unique performances with them. For a while, the personal styles and techniques of the various martial arts schools lead to hostile rivalries within the art form but as time has marched on, these rivalries have softened into friendly competition.

Today, the Lion Dance is a world famous art form. Its long history has taken it far from its shamanistic and Buddhist roots. It is now culture, ritual, art, entertainment and sports all rolled into one, a remarkable amalgamation of a wide range of influences. A living and evolving testament to the long history of the Chinese nation.

The modern Lion Dance has more "spice and flavour" to it.

Myths and Folklores

The shadowy and complex history of the Lion Dance is open to a fair amount of speculation as to its origins and evolution. It is almost impossible to know for sure exactly how the dance, as we know it, came to be. There are, however, a host of myths and legends from different regions and time periods that claim to tell the tale of its birth.

Many of the tales we are about to relate have significant elements in common, including the recurring theme of a beast that was the inspiration for the lion. It is not hard to imagine that all of these stories may have come from the same source and that they, like the dance, have evolved to reflect the place and time that they found themselves in. Though few of them recognise the incredibly long history and evolution of the dance that modern study has begun to reveal.

The Year Beast (*Nian Shou* 年獸)

This is one of the most famous tales. It tells of a strange beast, who in some versions emerges from under the sea and in other versions emerges from under a mountain to make an appearance in the same village every spring around Chinese New Year. Due to the yearly nature of its arrival and the strange noise that it made, which sounded like the word *Nian* 年, the Chinese word for 'Year', the villagers named it the 'Year Beast'.

The Beast was fearsome to behold with one eye and a large horn coming from its forehead but though it struck fear into the hearts of the villagers, who hid inside their homes whenever it appeared, it never did anyone any harm. Instead it would simply feed on the vegetation in the neighbouring fields. The problem was that this vegetation was the villagers' harvest!

One year, the villagers decided that they would no longer cower in their homes and that they would take action against the beast and attempt to save their produce. As the time for the Year Beast to make its appearance approached, the villagers worked to create a rival to chase the beast away. They made a head out of bamboo mesh over which they stuck many strips of colourful paper and they attached a large piece of triangular cloth to the head to act as a body.

As the Year Beast approached, two men wearing the costume rushed outside while the rest of the villagers aimed to make as much noise as they could by bashing on pots and pans. The terrified beast ran away, never to be seen again. Since then, the villagers re-enacted the ritual every spring to prevent the return of the Year Beast, which later became the basis for the Lion Dance as well as its association with Chinese New Year celebrations.

The story of the Nian Shou is one that is commonly used to explain the origins of the Lion Dance.

The Lion Tamer Monk

This legend is more closely connected with the Northern Lion Dance and it concerns a pair of tawny lions that lived in the Kunlun Mountains on the border between China and Tibet a thousand years ago. The lions were tremendously fierce and terrorised all the poor villagers who lived close to their territories. Many attempts to vanquish the pair had failed and it seemed that their reign of terror would never come to an end.

One day a high ranking monk, some people believe that he may have been the Buddha in disguise, came into the village. He claimed that he could succeed where so many others had failed. Though the villagers were incredulous, they let him try and indeed he made good on his claims. Not only did he manage to capture the lions, but he tied a red sash round each of their necks and led them down from the mountains as if they were his pets.

The Big-Headed Buddha and Jade Green Willow is a fixture in many Lion Dance performances.

The monk decided to present the two lions to the emperor as a gift. The emperor was so pleased with his lions that he made them the symbols of his empire. When the lions eventually died, the emperor was heartbroken, he commanded his finest craftsmen to fashion a pair of great golden lions that could be manipulated by two men in order to commemorate his fearsome companions. On special state occasions and at celebrations and festivals, the emperor would have the men perform a special Lion Dance to entertain his guests. This legend also accounts for the introduction of the Big-Headed Buddha (*Da Tou Fu* 大頭佛) character which sometimes accompanies the Lion Dance, he is thought to represent the monk who lead the lions down from the mountain.

The Envoy's Challenge

It is said that during the reign of Emperor *Zhangdi* 章帝 (75 – 88 A.D.), an envoy was sent from the nomadic *Yuezhi* peoples of the grasslands in the West. He brought the emperor the gift of a golden lion. This impressive gift was joined by a challenge however: the *Yuezhi* would only continue to pay tribute to the Han if they were able to tame the beast.

Emperor *Zhangdi* was initially convinced that the challenge would be child's play, as there must surely be someone among his great generals, or in his great empire, who would be strong enough to tame the beast. He was soon to find out, however, that the challenge was not so easily met as he had imagined. After two men had failed to bring the beast to heal, a third formed the theory that they could starve the animal into submission. At first the plan appeared to work as the lion became progressively weaker from lack of food, but as soon as he and his men tried to open the cage in order to prove that the lion had been tamed, the starving creature went wild. So great was the animal's fury, that they were unable to restrain it and rather than forfeit their own lives, they beat the lion to death.

Upon hearing of what had transpired, the emperor was furious. He threatened all those involved with execution. In fear of their lives the men came up with a solution. They skinned the lion and hid two men under the pelt to create the impression that the lion was, not only, still alive, but also beautifully tame.

Against all expectations their ruse worked. When the *Yuezhi* came to visit, at Chinese New Year, they were more than happy to accept that the lion had been tamed and to continue to pay their respects to the Han Empire. When news of the deception reached the people they were impressed and amazed and the Lion Dance was created to commemorate the event.

The *Foshan* Struggle

This legend is Cantonese in origin and the events it describes are believed to have taken place during the Qing Dynasty during the reign of Emperor *Qianlong* 乾隆 (1735 – 1796). It is the only legend listed here that accommodates for the involvement of martial arts in the choreography of the Lion Dance. As with some of the previous tales, the story begins when a fierce and powerful lion suddenly appears in the mountains.

The people of *Foshan* were being terrorised by a mighty lion. Three groups of martial artists had travelled into the mountains to try and defeat the beast but one by one each of the groups failed. Realising that the need to defeat the lion was greater than their individual rivalries, they sat down together to come with a new plan. They worked together to train the villagers so that they could all face the lion together as one great army. With their combined strength, the lion was quickly defeated.

In commemoration of their triumph, the villagers and martial artists together created an ornate lion costume and devised a victory dance that involved the martial arts moves that had helped them to be victorious. They went on to perform that dance every year so that their efforts would not be forgotten.

The incorporation of martial arts in Lion Dance was said to have been the result of a concerted effort by three groups to defeat a lion.

The Chinese Metaphysical Aspects

Dancing the Ritual

To understand the metaphysical significance of the Lion Dance, it is necessary to forget the modern understanding of dance simply as art and entertainment, and to remember that throughout the course of human history, dance and movement have often held far greater significance than we bestow upon them today. In ancient history, dance would have been, not just a matter of expression, but also a means of communication between man and the realms of spirits, gods and demons. Shamans, who would have acted as mediums between this world and the spiritual realms, would have used ritualised dance to build a bridge between the two and to bring the divine into the world of man.

Throughout man's earliest evolution and on into the development of bronze age cultures, the relationship between mankind and the natural world was a far more intimate one than we appreciate today. In the modern world, we regard shelter from the elements as a basic human right and we buy our food from the supermarket, we are closeted from the natural world in a hundred different ways. In the past, man's survival was entirely dependent on the capricious nature of the elements and on the success of the harvest and hunt. Early religion, understandably therefore focused around the empowerment of the natural world. Gods could be found in the weather, in the turning of the seasons and in the animals who interacted with man on a daily basis.

Animism and anthropomorphic personification was therefore a large part of religion as it would once have been practiced. Powers and abilities, virtues and vices, would be ascribed to certain animals and those animal gods would, it was believed, have had the power to influence the forces of nature to which early man would have been so vulnerable. In order to harness that power and use it to gain some measure of control over the natural world, humans would attempt to imitate animals through costume,

The Art of Lion Dance

This oracle bone pictograph of the character Wu 巫 depicts a person holding animals skins used in ritual.

movement and dance. The responsibility to harness that power and make contact with the divine, would have fallen to a shaman or "*Wu* 巫". He would have used ritual, movement, chanting and song to enter into a trance state that would allow him to see beyond the confines of the human realms into the greater worlds beyond.

Evidence of the pivotal nature of dance to the power of the shaman can be seen in the very construction of the character of "*Wu* 巫". "*Wu* 巫" depicts two persons (*Ren* 人) dancing around the character for work (*Gong* 工). So the central and defining role of the shaman was therefore to work to harness the power of dance to bring about positive change in human destiny. The word for dance itself, "*Wu* 舞", is pronounced in the same way as the word "*Wu* 巫" or shaman. Although these words have different tonal inflections, there are records in early Chinese literature of the two words being used interchangeably. The character for '*Wu* 舞' in turn depicts a dancer holding animal tails in each outstretched hand. This image itself is reminiscent of the shaman, dressed in animal skins, dancing in order to commune with the gods.

If you now work to picture a shaman in your mind's eye, you should see a man dancing into a state of ecstasy and exhaustion. You should also see a man dressed to resemble the animal whose power he hoped to harness. He would have worn an elaborate costume involving a headdress, if he was unable to use the skin of the animal that he wished to imitate, he would have constructed something that would resemble it as closely as he could manage.

He may also have painted his face to deepen the illusion that he was being transformed into the beast. This part of the ritual was called *Nuo Wu* 儺舞.

We can now see a series of powerful connections developing: between early religious belief and the power of animal gods, between the role of the shaman and the ritual of dance, between costume, music and the divine. Dance, particularly dance performed under the guise of being an animal, was a gateway to another world and the source of the shaman's power to change human destiny. Given the symbolism of the dance, it is not hard to see why the lion would quickly have been adopted as one of the animal gods that the shamans hoped to embody.

This pictograph of the character "dance" (Wu 舞) shows several people dancing around the character for work (Gong 工).

The lion is a particularly impressive beast. No matter where you live in the world, the lion is strongly associated with virtues of courage and bravery, power and strength. That association is particularly strong in China. If you go to the Forbidden City today, you will see a pair of magnificent bronze lions guarding the entrance to one of the palaces, and the Marco Polo Bridge is lined on each side with more than four hundred statues of lions. Even modern homes are sometimes guarded by stone lions who, it is hoped, will scare away ill fortune while lending an air of power and majesty to their surroundings.

As we have seen, it is entirely possible that the adoption of the lion as a symbol of power may have taken place as early as the Eastern Han, when the Chinese first encountered the lion as a court tribute. Once those in a position of power themselves had adopted such a symbol, it would not be long before their influence meant that that symbolism was taken up all over the nation. Given the tremendous impact that the lion had on the Chinese people when it was first encountered, and the awesome strength that it symbolises all over the world, even today, it is understandable therefore, that in a world in which animals could be gods, the lion would be understood to be a tremendously powerful god indeed. Alternatively, as the old shamanistic practices changed in the face of new belief systems and new influences like Buddhism, the old dances of power could have evolved and the original totemic animals been replaced by the fierce symbol of Emperor *Ashoka*.

The modern Lion Dance may be rather more sophisticated than the dances that would have been performed by shamans, but it is not hard to see that they carry with them the same heart and soul. Today's dancers still seek to portray the power and majesty of the beast through their powerful movements and through the elaborate nature of their costumes. They still seek to bring the animal to life through their movements, encouraging onlookers to suspend their disbelief and to be drawn into the performance, seeing before them a majestic lion rather than just two acrobats. We may no longer feel the need to harness the power of the lion god so keenly as we would once have done. We may no longer feel quite so at sea in the natural world, but centuries of tradition and spiritual understanding are still crystallised within the dance.

There are Lion Dance academies that still hold true to the beliefs and understanding that once coloured the Lion Dance. They still see the lion as more than spectacle. The lion is power and courage harnessed to become a guardian, a protector, a creator and a diviner. The lion god in service of man.

A shaman dresses up to embody the role of the animal they are representing.

Lion Dance and Qi Men Dun Jia

Qi Men Dun Jia 奇門遁甲 is an ancient form of divination that makes use of Chinese Metaphysics to harness the power in the universe. Like the Lion Dance itself, Qi Men originated in China but has spread its influence throughout the world, wherever the Chinese diaspora have taken root and come to call a place their home. Qi Men remains popular in Malaysia, Taiwan, Singapore and all over South East Asia as well as in mainland China. Qi Men has a host of potential applications from a straightforward use as a means for someone to influence their own personal fortunes to a tool in business planning, criminal investigations, missing persons cases and even military strategic planning. Alongside *Da Liu Ren* 大六壬 and *Tai Yi Shen Shu* 太乙神數, Qi Men is recognised as being one of the Three Arts (*San Shi* 三式) that are regarded as being China's highest metaphysical arts.

In first principles, Qi Men is a tool for mapping time, space and energy. It regards the time and energy continuum as being spread out over four realms, the Universe, the Heavens, Earth and Man, and across eight geographical directions. The mechanism through which this pattern of time and energy is mapped is incredibly detailed. The upshot of this is that Qi Men is not only able to predict the best possible day to perform a given action, but even the right hour, the perfect moment.

Qi Men is not magic. It cannot make miracles happen. But it can help an individual to be in the right place at the right time. It provides a guideline for practitioners to identify where and when there will be a positive convergence of Qi 氣 so that an individual may be better placed to feel inspired, energised and motivated and where a little good luck may be on their side. It is not, sadly, a substitute for hard work and natural talent but it may act as an amplifier, giving the individual an opportunity to make a greater impact than they could do on their own.

"How does this relate to the Lion Dance?", I hear you ask. As we have already outlined, the Lion Dance is more than sheer spectacle. It has its roots in shamanic practices and can be understood as a means of communicating with the divine. On a basic level, the Lion Dance serves to bring about good fortune on the one hand and to chase away negative fortune on the other. It may act to break negative cycles, chase away any bad luck that has been plaguing the onlooker and to change fortunes for the better. In Qi Men, it is believed that a simple human presence can be enough to activate the positive energy in a given sector. What if that presence is not simple however? What if that presence involves the awesome skill and energy of the Lion Dance with all the acrobatics, the rhythmic drums and the spectacle, the power of the lion itself? What could be achieved then?

In order to illustrate this possibility we will use an example. Imagine a small business owner, like a shopkeeper, his business has fallen on hard times, he is making a loss over and over again and no matter the effort that he put in, he cannot break out of that cycle of ill fortune. He is trapped in a pocket of negative Qi and there is apparently no escape. In Qi Men, we call this type of situation the Heavenly Web Earthly Net or *Tian Luo Di Wang* 天羅地網. To change his fortunes, this individual would need to break out of the web that binds them. This is where the lion can act as saviour.

Symbolic ingredients such as lettuce, mandarin oranges, pineapples, ingots and sometimes bottles, sugar or ropes are used to represent the obstacle. The lion's act of breaking into the formation and rescuing the trapped person symbolises hope and a change of luck and the triumph of the lion over the obstacles or negative forces (*Shi Wu Fu Mo* 獅舞伏魔).

Although the process itself is rather straightforward, it can be challenging to get to the starting point itself. Since there are various schools of Qi Men and metaphysics in existence, there

Symbolic ingredients such as lettuce, mandarin oranges, pineapples, ingots and sometimes bottles, sugar or ropes are used to represent the obstacle.

are various ways to carry out the dance. The most commonly used method prioritises the use of props such as mandarin oranges, pomelos, gold (to signify the trapped person's BaZi), tables or a paper net surrounding the gold (to signify the obstacles or prison), which belongs to the San Yuan school of Qi Men.

From a Qi Men perspective, the San Yuan system emphasises Qi management, for it is conceptualised on the balance between space and time. It uses the changes of the Five Elements to explain how all matters in this world can be affected by the change of space and time such as Qi flow. It emphasises the following four aspects: formation (*Xing* 形), universal principles (*Li* 理), for example, the Ba Gua and Five Elements, Qi (氣) and Numerology (*Shu* 數) – for example, time itself, time assessment and directional influence.

There is another school of thought known as the Image Number School (*Xiang Shu Pai* 象數派). Here the dance steps are plotted according to the Qi concept, and so they may not be visually attractive or exciting to watch due to the lack of props and formations and a decreased amount of interaction between the Lion and its environment. According to the traditions of this school, the Lion Dance troupe will perform their dance according to the right moves, and no more.

The Image Number School emphasises the theory that Qi flow is natural. The aim of this school is to indirectly guide one to a successful solution. Its focus remains on the aspects of materialisation and concentration, and within this context, the Lion Dance performers from the Image Number School often perform their routines based on instincts without set pattern and choreography.

It is unlikely that you will come across the Lion Dance being used for the kind of applications mentioned above. Few people now use the Lion Dance in conjunction with Qi Men at all and much of the knowledge has been lost. The Lion Dance has come to symbolise something rather more athletic and competitive than metaphysical. If you will give me the indulgence however, I will share with you a great historical event in which dance and Qi Men may well have been used together to create an outcome that has stood the test of time.

This story comes from the Three Kingdoms period in Chinese history, which ran from 220-280 A.D. The great military general *Zhuge Liang* 諸葛亮, called upon the east wind at his Seven Stars Altar (*Qi Xing Tan* 七星壇) in order that he may be able to defeat Cao Cao at the battle of the Red Cliffs. In acting as a Daoist theologian, *Zhuge Liang* would have dressed in certain ceremonial robes and he would have made use of props like flags, banners and spears. It is also entirely possible that the procession to his altar would have been a striking one, involving the beating of drums, the ringing of bells, certain styled steps and the use of elaborate swordplay or blade work. All of these factors would have combined together to allow him to access the metaphysical powers that he harnessed to such effect on that day. Could a Lion Dance or one of its early ancestors have been performed by the troops as they approached the altar with their hearts in their hands?

We have just begun to scratch the surface of the rich history behind the evolution of the Lion Dance. There is so much more that is yet to be explored in the pages of this book and so much more that we can learn about the ways in which the lion and metaphysics would once have been inseparable dance partners whose carefully choreographed steps would have been used to change the fates of man. Whether you have any interest in Feng Shui or Qi Men or whether your interest is solely in Chinese history and heritage, it is my hope that you will learn a great deal about the true depth and significance of the Lion Dance as a part of Chinese culture and if you are interested in Chinese Metaphysics, maybe it will change the way you look at the Lion Dance altogether. If you ever choose to hire a Lion Dance troupe, maybe you will give thought to more than the spectacle. Maybe you will think about the ethos and the belief system of the troupe that you hire and in fully embracing the rich history of the Lion Dance, maybe you will be able to harness the power of lion to change your world for the better.

Zhuge Liang was a well-known practitioner of Qi Men Dun Jia.

Chapter 2

The Lion And The Craft

There are a great number of different elements that come together to create the spectacle of the Lion Dance: choreography, music, rhythm and sheer acrobatic skill and athleticism. The Lion Dance is truly a team effort. Crowning all of these, and really bringing the lion to life, is the costume. The lion head in particular is of paramount importance to the life and the expression in the animal.

The creation of the lion head has been through as much of an evolution as the dance itself. The heads, as we see them today, are the culmination of hundreds of years of artistry and innovation. The craftsmanship involved in creating the lion head is an art form in itself and is recognised as being a National Intangible Cultural Heritage in China.

Throughout much of history, the lion head would have been made by the dancers themselves, but today it can be the focus of an individual's career. Most of the manufacturing of lion heads takes place in Guangdong province but other countries, like Malaysia, are known to manufacture their own. The lion heads are a particularly interesting aspect of the performance, as they are one of the ways in which the regional identity of the dance and the dancers can be recognised.

While the choreography of most Lion Dances is thought to fall broadly into the category of Northern Lion (*Bei Shi* 北獅) the Southern Lion (*Nan Shi* 南獅), the lion head reveal far more subtlety and variation. If one looks closely, there are four major styles of the lion head: the Closed-mouth Lion (*Guan Kou Shi* 關口獅), the Opened-mouth Lion (*Kai Kou Shi* 開口獅), the Northern (*Bei Shi* 北獅) or Peking Lion (*Bei Jing Shi* 北京獅) and the Southern (*Nan Shi* 南獅) or Cantonese Lion, (*Guang Dong Shi* 廣東獅). This is, however, just the tip of the iceberg and there are many more derivatives and subtle variations that exist under each one of these general headings.

A craftsman putting on the final touches to a lion head.

The Art of Lion Dance

Closed-mouth Lion

Closed-mouth Lion
(Guan Kou Shi 關口獅)

The Closed-mouth Lion, as you might have guessed, is recognisable because its mouth is closed. This is actually quite unusual as most lion heads have an open mouth that can be manipulated as a part of the performance. The Closed-mouth Lion instead has a mouth that is moulded, painted and immobile.

It is believed that the lion head would initially have been fashioned out of a kind of concave rattan or bamboo basket, a method which is still used in Taiwan today, and that over time these woven heads were replaced by carved wooden heads and ultimately by the *papier-mâché* heads made popular by *Yang Xian Qiang* during the Song Dynasty (910 – 1279).

Traditionally, these *papier-mâché* lion heads would first have been moulded out of clay and that clay cast would then have been used as the basis from which to craft the *papier-mâché* version. The clay head would have been modelled after the stylised heads of lions used on door knockers, incense cauldrons or statues. Once completed, the forehead would be marked with the Chinese character "王" or "*Wang*", which means king, while the back of its head is painted with the *Ba Gua* 八卦 and *Tai Ji* 太極 symbols. The eyes would be represented by small wooden balls affixed inside of the eye sockets with wire. An alternative method may have been for a soldier to use his shield as the mask, painting on the necessary features.

Of course no traditional art form is ever free of the march of time and today many Closed-mouth Lions are made by machine in factories. These conveyor built lion heads tend to be made out of cardboard or aluminium. Cardboard lions tend to lack in durability, therefore, they are seldom used in performances. They are far more likely to be sold as decorative items, talismans or children's toys.

The Art of Lion Dance

Opened-mouth Lion
(Kai Kou Shi 開口獅)

In most respects, the Opened-mouth Lion closely resembles the Closed-mouth Lion. The eyes and most of the other main features are very similar. The difference, of course, being in the creation of the mouth. The Opened-mouth Lion does not just have an open-mouthed or roaring expression, the mouth of lion can actually be manipulated by the dancers; opening and closing to lend further expression to the beast as the dance unfolds.

Opened-mouth Lions

These surface similarities however belie and tremendous difference in the way that the two styles of head are manufactured. While Closed-mouth Lions are often mass produced using machines and are frequently fashioned from aluminium, Open-mouthed Lions are exclusively manufactured using traditional methods. Manufacturers of Opened-mouth Lions believe that the aluminium versions are unwieldy and difficult to carry. The opening and closing of an aluminium mouth also makes a clashing sound like the sound of clashing swords. Open-mouth Lions are still therefore built using a bamboo frame.

Opened-mouth Lions are also often decorated slightly differently from their Closed-mouth cousins. In place of the character "王" or "Wang" on the forehead, there is a small round mirror and above the symbol for Ba Gua on the back of the lion head, there appears a representation of the Seven Stars of the Big Dipper (Qi Xing Tu 七星圖). This very much brings the Southern Lion in line with Daoist spiritual traditions. These are also the same Seven Stars that are referenced in Qi Men.

Despite the differences in the construction of the heads, these main types of lions will have very similar body shapes consisting of a large piece of cloth. This cloth would originally have been made out of plant fibres but Modern Lions are more likely to be clothed in velvet or linen. Both lions will also have a bushy tail which can be made out of a variety of different materials including hemp, yarn and even real fur.

The colours of the lions may also tell a tale which only those in-the-know will be able to decipher. The traditional colours that would have been used reflected the Five Elements and the Five Directions and would have conveyed specific messages within the context of a Qi activation ritual. The various decorations all equally have a specific meaning that goes well beyond mere aesthetics. Sadly in the modern world much of this has been forgotten and many dance schools, while still using the traditional decorations, colour their dragons according to their tastes.

Northern Lion (*Bei Shi* 北獅)

The Northern Lion is perhaps one of the most easily distinguishable lion heads in use today due to its furry appearance. In comparison to its southern counterpart which has a stylised face, the Northern Lion has a more defined and expressive face. Since it rather resembles a Pekingese or Fu dog, it is also commonly called the Peking Lion (*Bei Jing Shi* 北京獅), although sometimes other names such as Furry Lion (*Mao Shi* 毛獅), Golden Lion (*Jin Shi* 金獅) or Green Lion (*Qing Shi* 青獅) are also used.

The Northern Lion is likely derived from wooden-headed lions used in the Tang dynasty as court entertainment before the time of *Master Yang Xian Qiang* 楊顯搶, who lived in the Northern Song dynasty (960 – 1127 A.D.). *Master Yang* adopted the model, revolutionised the construction techniques and incorporated martial arts into the dance. Subsequent periods in Hebei province saw further improvements made to *Master Yang*'s model which eventually evolved into the current Northern Lion form widely used today.

The techniques for making the Northern Lion's head is not unlike that of the Opened-mouth Lion, although the former is uniquely shaped in a pyramidal or conical form which culminates in a rounded protuberance at the top of its head – an influence from Buddhist elements which recalls a similar feature called an *ushnisha* on the Buddha's head. These Buddhist features however are no longer common in China and the head is now left smooth. The entire head is painted in gold with other facial features such as eyes, mouth and teeth painted in different colours.

The eyes are movable glass balls with bushy eyebrows and the ears are large and floppy. The entire lion including the body is painstakingly conveyed as a whole piece through the clever usage of fine hemp or nylon fur dyed in yellow which covers the gaps between the headpiece and body. The illusion is further enhanced

Northern Lions

by chest-high trousers of similar material on the performers. All these fine details serve to give the lion a life-like appearance during a performance.

In a performance of two Northern Lions, the gender of the lions is distinguishable from one another. A female lion is tied with a green-coloured ribbon while the male with a red-coloured ribbon. Alternatively, the colour of the fur on the lion head and back may also indicate its gender with green or red ribbon. However, in recent days, dancers have taken liberty with the colours.

The performance of the Lion Dance encapsulates active, happy and playful movements. The playfulness of the dance is conveyed by the dancers' moves which border on gymnastics; rolling or wrestling with one another, leaping over furniture, actively jumping and climbing after a ball, all of which involve vigorous movements.

Southern Lion (Nan Shi 南獅)

The Southern Lion is largely considered to be the most popular version of the dance. It is by far the most recognised on an international stage and is easily recognisable due to its eye-catching colours and unique performances. The title of Southern Lion was earned simply because of the regions where it became most popular but it has been known by a variety of different titles as the centuries have passed by.

One of the earliest titles for the dance may well have been "*Rui Shi* 瑞獅" which means "Auspicious Lion" which is connected with one of the many origin tales which surround the Lion Dance. This tale was popular in the *Foshan* region, and dates back to the Qing Dynasty. It describes how Emperor *Qianglong* 乾隆, who ruled from 1736 until 1796, and his entourage became lost in the woods but were lead to safety by a strange beast with a horn upon its head. This title was popular until as late as 1928 when a reawakening of patriotic fervour lead to a renaming of the lion.

佛山
Foshan

鶴山
Heshan

In 1928 foreign incursions were made into the city of *Ji Nan* 濟南 by the British and by the Japanese. The Chinese population were outraged and students took to the streets in protest throughout the city of Guangzhou 廣州. These protests soon broke into violence as the invading powers took steps to aggressively suppress the dissenting voices. There were many deaths that day and the united outrage of a nation lead to the renaming of the Lion Dance. The word '*Rui*' sounds similar to the word "*Shui* 睡" which means "sleep", it was believed that this title sounded too passive and the Chinese wanted it to be understood that they were not to be trifled with. The new name for the Southern Lion was to be "*Xing Shi* 醒獅" which means 'Awakened Lion'.

Over time, the overwhelming popularity of the dance in the regions of Guangzhou and Hong Kong, coupled with the popularity of Hong Kong cinema throughout the 1990s, lead to the Southern Lion being inseparably connected with these areas on a global stage. For this reason, the Southern Lion, is now often referred to as the Cantonese Lion.

The performance of the Southern Lion is very much focused around the horse stance. A powerful martial arts pose in which the performer stands with his feet apart and his knees bent. From this basic stylistic point, the performance further diverges into two distinct schools of performance: the *Foshan* 佛山 School and the *Heshan* 鶴山 School. These schools are named after the cities in which the costumes for their performances are generally manufactured. The *Foshan* 佛山 School takes a very traditional approach to the dance, while the *Heshan* 鶴山 School is more relaxed and innovative in its style.

Southern Lions

Design of the Southern Lion

The construction of the Southern Lion begins with the construction of a bamboo frame held together with gauze paper. This frame is then tied to a series of sturdy rattan rings and is then further reinforced with the use of bamboo bands. This structure is given stability and held together by wooden braces. This frame is then covered with a layer of wet gauze which is allowed to dry before being covered with another layer of gauze and then another. The final step in the process is to cover the gauze with plaster which is then sanded down and painted.

The shape that the lion head takes on is dictated by the style of the dance that it is to be used for. The *Foshan* 佛山 School uses a head that is wide and round with a short wide mouth piece that gives the impression that the lion is smiling just a touch. This head is then decorated with very bright colours and the idea is to create a lion that appears to be lively and alert.

The *Heshan* 鶴山 School uses a head that is taller and narrower with a mouthpiece that protrudes from the head like a duck's bill. For this reason the *Heshan* Lion is often referred to as "*Ya Zui Shi* 鴨嘴獅" which means "Duckbill Lion". The shape of the head also means that it is sometimes mistaken for a Hakka *Qi Lin* 麒麟 which is popularly referred to as the Chinese Unicorn.

The traditional colour schemes for Cantonese lions are inspired by Chinese Opera makeup, specifically that of *Liu Bei* and his Five Tiger Generals (*Wu Hu Jiang* 五虎將). The colours used are also associated with the Five Elements: Yellow correlates with Earth, Red with Fire, Black with Water, Green with Wood and White with Metal. The combinations of colours that are used, convey different messages. Traditional Kung Fu schools are bound by the unwritten

Heshan Lion

Southern Lion

rules of history and will decorate their dragons in a distinct fashion but many other dance companies will take a more liberal view and value aesthetics over other considerations.

You may not be aware that the lions are also depicted at different life stages and that these life stages carry with them different degrees of seniority. The oldest lions are primarily white with long beards, gold or yellow is used for middle aged lions and the younger lions are black. All lions will however be the same size apart from the very young lions, (*Shao Shi* 少獅 or *Yao Shi* 幼獅), these smaller lions are typically carried by children who are being introduced to the art of the Lion Dance and they are usually decorated in bright colours and given a rather cuter more playful appearance.

The Art of Lion Dance

Liu Bei Lion

Liu Bei Lion 劉備獅

The *Lui Bei* Lion represents the Emperor of the *Han Shu*. He embodies power, wisdom and benevolence and is the most auspicious of the lions. This lion is traditionally yellow or gold in colour with white eyebrows and a long beard. The three cold coins that appear on the back of this head represent the fact that he is the eldest of three brothers. It is generally only Masters of the Art, and Kung Fu schools with very long histories, who will dance with a lion of this nature. The longer the beard, the more respect is denoted to the *Shi Fu* who wields the lion, an excessively long beard indicates that this *Shi Fu* commands the respect of the entire Kung Fu community.

Guan Yu Lion

Guan Yu Lion 關羽獅

The *Guan Yu* or *Guan Gong* Lion is junior to the *Lui Bei* Lion but, as he represents one of *Liu Bei*'s most remarkable generals, he is thought to stand for the qualities of bravery and loyalty. This lion traditionally has a red face and a black body, his beard is either white or black, and not as long as that of the *Liu Bei* Lion. This lion has two gold coins on the back of his head indicating that he is the second of three brothers. Anyone can use the *Guan Yu* lion which means it is one of the lions most people will recognise, lions such as this will often be seen performing at corporate functions and business events.

Zhang Fei Lion

Zhang Fei Lion 張飛獅

The *Zhang Fei* Lion represents bravery and leadership. It is known as the Battle or Fighting Lion and is distinctive in that it is typically painted black with white patterns, has a metal horn, battered ears and a black beard and eyebrows. He is the youngest of the three brothers and has only one gold coin on the back of his head. He is usually portrayed as being irascible, quick to anger and ever ready for a fight.

Huang Zhong Lion

Huang Zhong Lion 黃忠獅

The *Huang Zhong* Lion is often referred to as the Righteous Lion and it is associated with qualities of perseverance, kindness and stability. The general after whom it is named fought in a conflict that lasted for three generations without faltering, ultimately achieving victory through his enduring courage. This lion has a yellow face and body and a long silver beard.

The Art of Lion Dance

Zhao Yun Lion

Zhao Yun Lion 趙雲獅

This lion has a green face and its body is usually white with green, black or yellow streaks. It is named after *Zhao Yun* 趙雲, a tremendously successful military general, and this lion is thought to be both competitive and fearless. He is also known as the Heroic Lion.

Ma Chao Lion

Ma Chao Lion 馬超獅

This lion is known as the filial lion. According to the tales told, General *Ma Chao* 馬超 always wore a white armband when fighting against *Cao Cao*, the Emperor of Wei. It was in memory of his father and brother who were both murdered by his enemy. For this reason the lion is always decorated in white and is used only at the funeral of a "Master (*Shi Fu* 師傅)" or other important leaders. This lion is usually built expressly for purpose and is burned after the service for fear that its association with death may bring ill fortune upon those who keep it.

Notable Regional Forms

Vietnamese Lion

The Vietnamese 'Lion Dance' is not really a Lion Dance at all. Despite the similarity to the Chinese Lion Dance, the beast that performs in Vietnam is not believed to be a lion at all but a unicorn. According to legend, the unicorn appeared in Vietnam for the first time in 600 A.D. and it is thought to represent peace, prosperity and happiness. The Vietnamese Unicorn Dance is similarity choreographed around acrobatics and martial arts and, like its Chinese counterpart, is thought to drive away ill fortune and bring more auspicious luck in its wake. One interesting feature of the Vietnamese dance, that makes it truly unique, is the presence of *Ong Dia*, or the spirit of the Earth, represented by a grinning man with a pot belly who carries a palm leaf. *Ong Dia* acts to summon the unicorn and to clear a path for it to dance unhindered.

Vietnamese Lions

Japanese Lion

The Japanese Lion Dance is known as *Shishimai*. It is thought to have entered Japan from China and it originally featured just one dancer but, over time, a two man version evolved and now both versions of the dance can be seen being performed all over the country, the one dancer version being particularly popular in Eastern Japan. Though we tend to think immediately of China when we think about the Lion Dance, it is interesting to note that the dance is so popular in Japan that there are thought to be more than 9000 different regional variations, each one distinct in appearance from each of the others.

The lion in Japan, like the lion in China, is thought to chase away ill fortune but it is also thought to protect crops and is frequently used as a part of harvest celebrations. The head of the lion is usually made out of lacquered wood, with the body of the beast being represented by a piece of green cloth decorated with white designs.

Japanese Lion

Korean Lion

The Korean Lion Dance is known as *Sanye* and there are two main variations of the dance that survive in Korea today: *Saja-noreum* and *Sajach'um*. The first of these two is an exorcism drama which features a brown lion and reflects the lion mask play from *Bukchong*. This lion is joined by a host of other dancers and performers, including a vast array of musicians playing gongs, flutes and double-headed drums. This lion will dance at night for the first fifteen nights of the lunar New Year. The second of the two lions is used to perform in masked dramas and is typically white. What makes these lions particularly distinct is their open mouth and lolling tongue.

Korean Lions

Tibetan (Snow) Lion

The Lion Dance of the Himalayas and Tibet is unique in that it features a Snow Lion that reflects the snowy mountains and glaciers that typify the region. The dance is called *Senggeh Garcham* and it features a white lion with sleepy eyes and a turquoise mane. Popular throughout the Himalayas as well as among the *Monpa* people in Arunachal Pradesh and in *Sikkim*, the *Senggeh Garcham* is a ritual dance of the *Bon Po* monks but most people see it performed for purely entertainment purposes. The Snow Lion is thought to represent power, strength, courage and joy, as well as the Earth element.

Tibetan (Snow) Lion

Modern Interpretations

The Lion Dance has changed and evolved over time and these changes are very apparent in the costume design. Both the appearance and the manufacturing processes involved in the creation of lion costumes have changed drastically over the years. These alterations reflect both the evolution of modern technology and changing sensibilities towards the more traditional aspects of the dance.

As we have discussed, the head of the lion is now made in a very different fashion than would once have been the case. In the very early days, the variety of tools and materials available to use in the construction of the head were limited. They would have been formed entirely out of carved wood and the appearance of the mask was often far more rustic and less stylised than it is the custom today. To a modern eye, these lion heads would likely look quite fierce, while current lion heads are rather more refined and delicate looking, involving far more intricate details around the eyes, eyelids and mouth.

Further massive changes took place when the art of creating lion heads became popular in Malaysia, gaining momentum in the 1970s before reaching a crescendo in the 1990s. The Malaysians began to use sheepskin to create bushy eyebrows and moustaches, as well as laser paper, a kind of reflective metallic paper, to create the lion's skin. Laser paper is now popularly used in gold and silver, as well as red, green, blue and purple.

醒獅

Various modern Southern Lion heads

Likewise, the bodies, or 'lion tails (*shi wei* 獅尾)', have also changed a tremendous amount. In the past, the body could have been anywhere from ten feet right up to fifteen feet in length and regardless of the colour of the head, it would have been dyed a cornucopia of different rainbow colours. Modern bodies tend to be much smaller, only seven to eight feet in length, and the rainbow colours have been rejected in favour of a rather more stylised appearance that uses only one or two colours to reflect the decoration on the head. The fabric used has also changed over the years. While the original lion's bodies would have been made of silk, Modern Lions tend to be made out of more durable modern fibres like nylon or Mylar, if a more reflective or shiny appearance is preferred.

The shorter tails were originally introduced in Singapore in the late sixties. The thought process at the time was that a shorter body would more closely resemble a real lion, but the knock on effect was that the shorter bodies were easier to manoeuvre and control. This meant that the shorter tails became popular all over, particularly for competitive lions.

Modern Lion Dance costumes nowadays do not strictly follow traditional colour schemes and come in all sorts designs.

Though longer tails are still sometimes used in celebrations and where tradition is valued, the shorter tails are now considered to be more aesthetically pleasing, as well as practical. The Southern Lion also began to make use of the shorter tails and to take on some of the costume aspects of the Northern Lion. In particular, the use of matching trousers for the dancers and faux claws.

Modern Lions tend to be more creative in their use of colour, while simultaneously being more sophisticated in their design than their traditional counterparts. On the one hand, traditional colours are used in a more creative fashion or overlooked altogether in favour of a vast array of modern hues. On the other hand, a greater degree of uniformity and colour coordination is expected between the decoration of the head and the body.

Where traditional colours are still used, there is far more flexibility in the way that those colours are employed. Colours are matched in alternative patterns and, where rules may once have been quite rigid, there is now more flexibility. For instance, there was once a tradition that the lion's nose should be green and his horn should always be black representing iron, these kinds of very prescriptive rules no longer apply.

Where less traditional colours are used, the sky may appear to be the limit, but there are still expectations with regard to the sophistication of the design. The manufacturing of lions in Malaysia has led to a host of local flavours being added to lion designs, such as batik. There are also gold lions and silver lions – representing wealth, neon lions, and even lions which feature LED lights. Even within this cornucopia of possibilities, the head and the body will be expected to be carefully colour matched and brought together in an all-encompassing design. For instance, if the lion was silver and purple, these two main shades would be prevalent throughout the design of the lion from beginning to end: the paintwork might be purple and the body might be decorated with silver scales overlaid with sheer purple fabric, the pompoms would be purple and the overall look would be a very polished one.

Modern Lions are a marvel. They are bold, beautiful and truly spectacular entertainment. If, however, your interest in the Lion Dance is more metaphysical in nature, it still may be worth giving thought to adopting a more traditional design.

Constructing the Lion

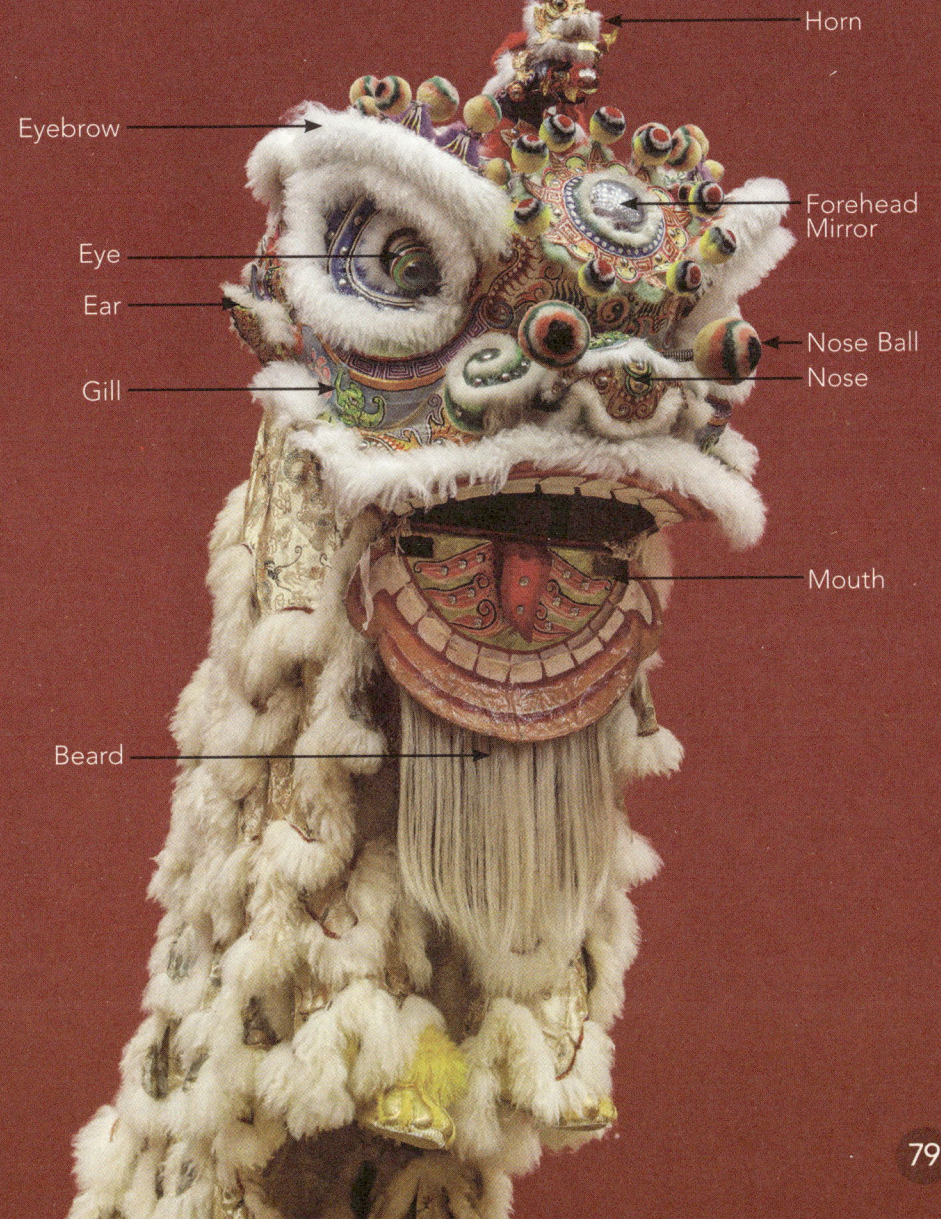

- Horn
- Eyebrow
- Eye
- Ear
- Gill
- Forehead Mirror
- Nose Ball
- Nose
- Mouth
- Beard

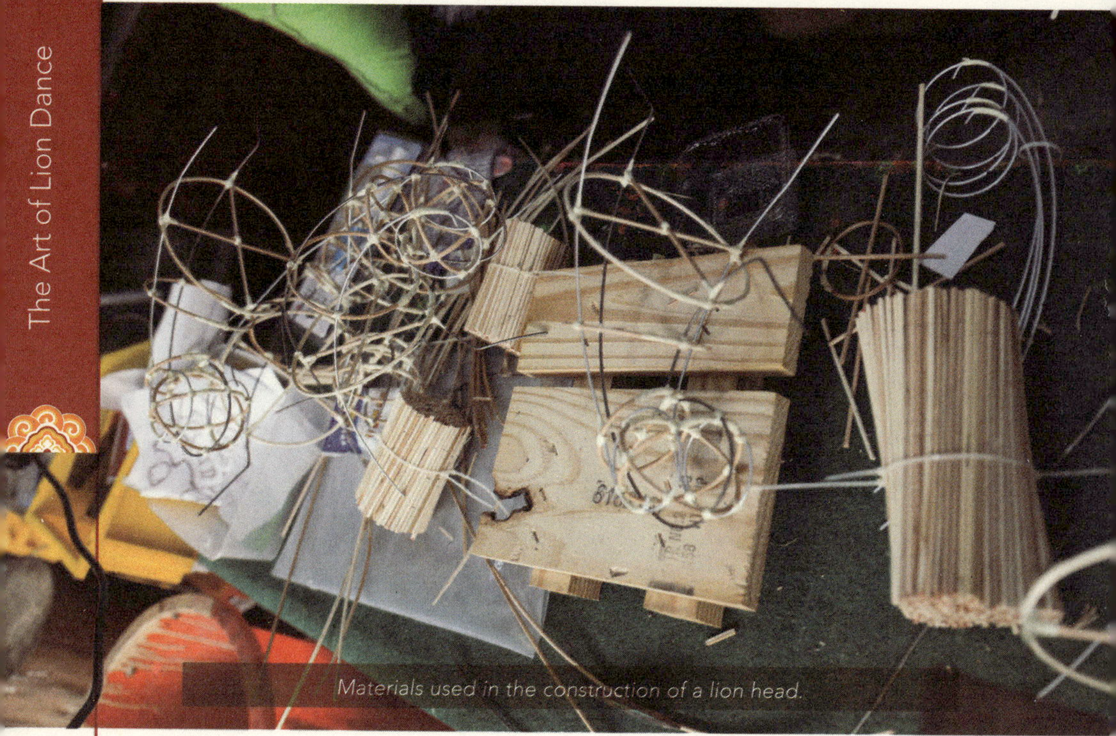

Materials used in the construction of a lion head.

i) Preparing the materials

There is a Chinese proverb which states that "A craftsman must first sharpen his tools before he will be able to succeed at the task (*gong yu shan qi shi, bi xian li qi qi* 工欲善其事，必先利其器)". Preparation, as we all know, is the key to succeeding in most walks of life. To begin to construct a lion, therefore, it is necessary to have the right materials to hand.

The most important materials for constructing the lion head are bamboo strips and gauze paper. Bamboo is used for the construction of the head because it is strong, light and flexible all at once. The gauze paper is then used to paper over the frame. Other essential materials are: iron wire, glue water, laser paper, acrylic paints, calligraphy brushes, horsehair, wool, sheepskin, and hot-melt adhesive.

Constructing the bamboo frame around the aluminium bottom frame.

ii) Framing

This is the first step in creating the lion head. It is said that the lion head should be able to withstand pressure of ten times its own weight without distorting, but it will generally only weigh about 4 kg in total and should be easy to manoeuvre. This is by far the most important stage as it creates the basic structure upon which everything else must rest. If a fault is found when the next stage begins, there is no way to correct it, so the craftsman needs to get it right first time.

This stage is complex and challenging. It is a painstaking process that must be undertaken with great care and precision. It is a true art rather than a science, however, and there are no hard and fast rules than can be followed. Each craftsman must carefully learn what is required from his teacher and only experience will teach him how to gauge the right measurements and proportions.

Building the bamboo frame.

The frame of a lion head is built of bamboo strips and iron wires affixed around a one inch flat aluminium bar than forms a semi-rounded base frame. The bamboo strips are brought together to form the shape of the head and it is considered to be of paramount importance that there is a clear and accurate centre mark to the head so that it can be perfectly symmetrical.

There are a number of features that are important in the construction of the head, and these features will vary depending on the kind of lion that is being constructed. For instance a standard Southern Lion will have a plump forehead (*shi tou ba man* 獅頭飽滿), smooth overall shape (*xian tiao liu chang* 線條流暢), wide smiling mouth (*kou kuo dai xiao* 口闊帶笑), big bright eyes (*yan da ming liang* 眼大明亮), amygdaline nose (*xing bi* 杏鼻) and bright teeth (*ming ya zhen chi* 明牙震齒).

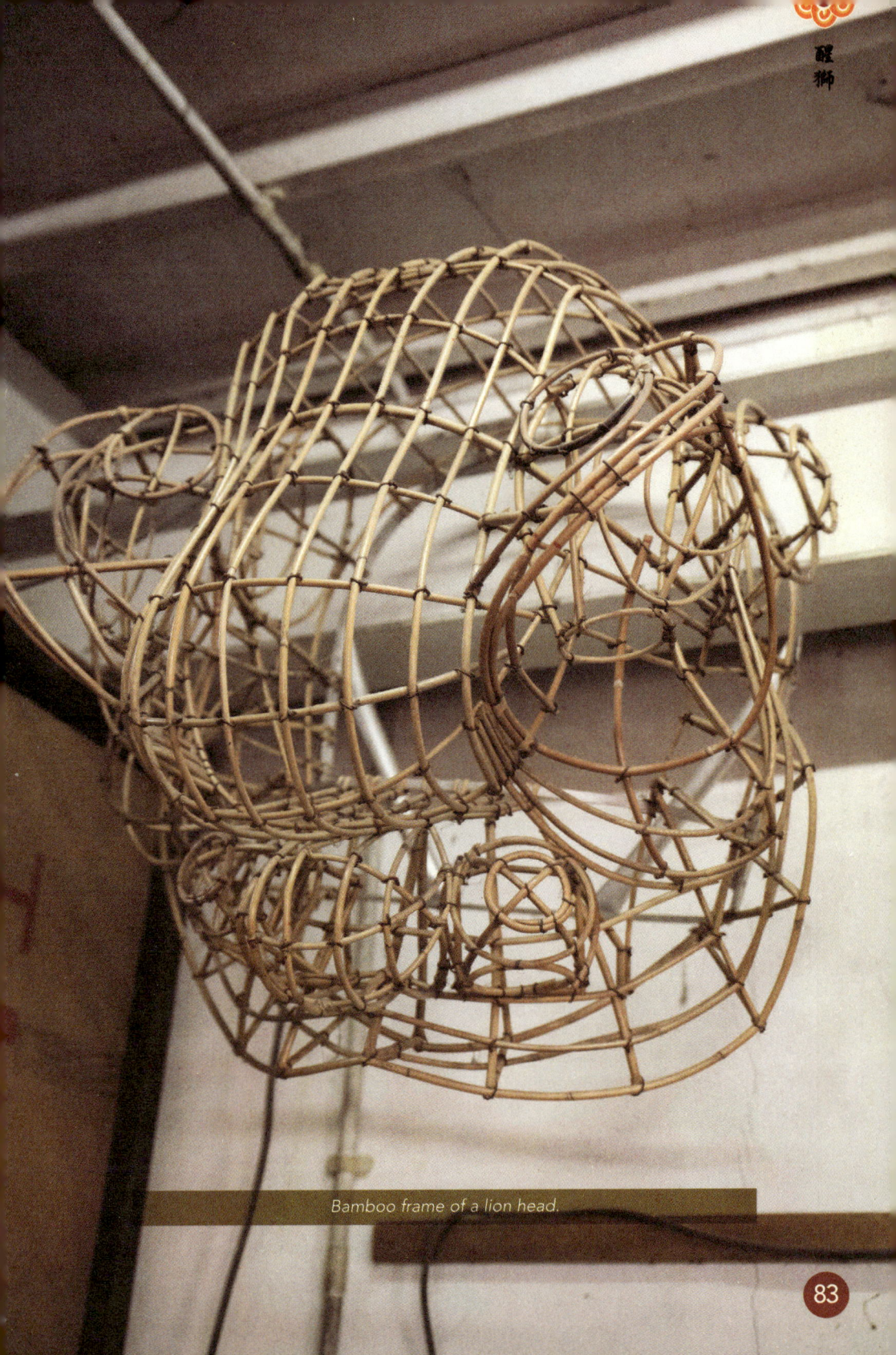

Bamboo frame of a lion head.

Some of the features that involve extra care and attention are as follows:

- **The Lion's Forehead (***Shi E* 獅額**)**

    The forehead of the lion is usually 58.3 cm high and there are two styles of forehead that may be used, depending on the kind of lion that is being build: the plump forehead lion (*bao e shi* 飽額獅) and convex forehead lion (*tu e shi* 凸額獅). The plump forehead lion has a wide circular forehead that is thought to represent simplicity and purity. This kind of forehead is used in the construction of a *Liu Bei* Face (*Liu Bei Mian* 劉備面)". The convex forehead is instead thought to represent more aggressive and pugnacious character traits and is seen on the red "*Guan Yu* Face (*Guan Yu Mian* 關羽面)" and the black "*Zhang Fei* Face (*Zhang Fei Mian* 張飛面)".

- **The Lion's Back (***Shi Bei* 獅背**)**

    This does not refer to the fabric that represents the lion's body but to the back of the lion head. This tends to be rather streamlined and sleek in shape. It is also important that this section of the head contains some internal padding for the comfort of the performer that is wearing the mask.

- **The Lion's Mouth (***Shi Kou* 獅口)

  The mouth is a very important feature. There is a great deal of character that can be contained within the set of the mouth. A lion's mouth, as we have discussed, can be either mobile or fixed. It is also quite the focal feature when it comes to the part of the dance where the lion eats the ceremonial greens during *Cai Qing* 採青.

- **The Lion's Eyebrow (***Shi Mei* 獅眉)

  It is surprising how often we overlook the importance of eyebrows even to a human face. Eyebrows, however, do more than highlight the positioning of the eyes. There is a great deal of expression and personality to be found in eyebrows and it is no different with a lion head.

- **The Lion's Horn (***Shi Jiao* 獅角)

  To the uninitiated, there may not appear to be a tremendous amount that can be done with the lion's horn, but you would be surprised by the variety of different designs that can be employed. Each style of head has its own unique horn: the "Eagle Beak Horn (*Ying Jiao* 鷹角)", "Sharp Horn (*Jian Jiao* 尖角)", "Elephant Trunk Horn (*Xiang Bi Jiao* 象鼻角)", "Bull Horn (*Niu Jiao* 牛角)" and "Tiger Fang Horn (*Hu Jiao* 虎角)".

iii) Papering and Masking

The next stage in the process involves covering the frame with gauze, gauze paper and glue water to create the completed shape of the lion, ready to be painted. The entire frame is covered both inside and out in order to reinforce the head, form the features of the lion and to protect the frame.

The first layer to be put in place is a layer of gauze brushed with diluted glue. The glue performs the dual purpose of sticking the gauze to the frame, while simultaneously stiffening the cloth to form a rigid base layer which can be used to shape the important features of the head. After this foundation layer is in place, it is overlaid with gauze paper and this layering process continues until there are between three and six layers in place.

Covering the framework with layers of gauze and paper.

To complete the process, a layer of laser paper is used to create a smooth and shiny finish that is easy to paint. This final stage is called 'masking' and is a modern invention. In the past, the gauze itself would have been dyed in a variety of bright colours, now that injection of colour, and indeed a sparkly or iridescent quality, is given by the laser paper.

Each one of these layers must dry completely before the next layer can be put in place. This can take up to two hours in a shaded outdoor space or well-ventilated room which can make this part of the process a lengthy one.

A lion head which has been fully papered.

Partially painted lion heads.

iv) Painting

The elaborate decorative patterns on the lion heads are heavily focused around calligraphy and this is an important skill in any craftsman wishing to learn to make a lion costume. Alongside the calligraphy are a range of traditional patterns and colour schemes. The colours chosen for the painting of the dragons are connected with themes of luck, happiness and joy and their origins can be found in Chinese culture and tradition. The patterns are also are intended to convey auspicious hopes and wishes and these include patterns of dots, spirals and flames.

Modelling patterns before the painting process.

The heads are painted freehand, there are no stencils or guides for the craftsmen to use, so they must rely solely on their talents and their steady hands. The work is painstaking and meticulous. Each craftsman must exercise extreme care to ensure that the intricate patterns are perfectly placed on the lion head and appropriately scaled and colour matched – creating a finished product that is balanced and beautiful.

Preparing paints for the colouring process.

Unsurprisingly, craftsmen must practise for some time before they will be permitted to perform the most challenging parts of the work. The painting is usually, therefore, performed in three stages reflecting the degrees of skill required at each level. The first stage, mapping the outline of the pattern onto the head, is performed only by the most senior craftsmen. The second stage involves filling in these outlines and giving the pattern colour and depth, this is given to the intermediate craftsmen. The final stage is given to junior craftsmen and this involves checking through the finished pattern to ensure that there are no mistakes and to touch up or fill in anything that looks out of balance.

Putting the finishing touches to a lion's eyebrows.

v) Decorating

The final stage adds the details that really bring the lion head to life. First of all, dyed wool and sheepskin are attached to the lion's forehead, mouth, horn, nose, eyes and eyelids using hot-melt adhesive. This forms the eyebrows, eyelashes and beard, as well as highlighting some of the most important features.

Next the lion's lower jaw and chin are tied to the rest of the head so they can be freely moved and manipulated. The eyeballs are also attached into the eye sockets using wire, and silk pompoms are attached to the sides of each nostril.

The final decoration to be put in place is arguably one of the most important. This is a mirror that is placed on the lion's forehead. It is thought to represent praying to the Buddha and reflects the Buddhist influences that may have contributed to the development of the dance as we know it. Once this last item has been glued in place, the lion head is left in a shaded and cool outdoors space or in a well-ventilated room to dry.

Making the Lion's Body

There is generally more than one fabric chosen to create the body of the lion and these are cut into long wavy sections that are stitched together in the right shape and size to be able to fall over the backs of the dancers. The fabrics are generally brightly-coloured and quite heavy in texture, they are almost always chosen in contrasting colours that coordinate well with the design of the lion head. Popular fabrics are satin and sequined cloth, the choice of fabric is frequently shiny like the modern finish of the head.

Once the overall shape is in place, the fabric will be decorated. Patterns involving points, lines, curves and circular patterns are all popular and most craftsman will also stitch on a shining fish scale pattern to really make the lion sparkle. The middle of the fabric is then elasticated to help it keep its shape and drape without affecting the movement of the dancers.

The body is attached to the head using Velcro. The benefit of Velcro as opposed to a more permanent means of attachment is that the body can be easily removed and cleaned or even replaced, if it becomes damaged. Once the body is securely in place, the lion is complete. However, this will not take place until the lion is officially brought to life in the 'Awakening Ceremony' (*Kai Guang Dian Jing* 開光點睛).

Dotting the mirror at the lion's forehead during the consecration or "Kai Guang" ceremony.

Consecrating or "Awakening" the Lion

All lions, and especially the 'Awakened' ones, are afforded a tremendous amount of respect. They are not considered to be simply costumes. The reverence extended to a lion is more akin to that which would be extended to a sanctified image or statue of a deity. Although the lion is not considered to be a god exactly, it is thought to be a representative of heaven and, as such, is still a divine being. The lion is closer to heaven and therefore higher than man, it is always handled with extreme care even when not in use and it is not considered to be 'alive' until it has been 'Awakened' or consecrated.

The 'Awakening' of the lions is thought to connect them with the heavens and allow them to fully embody their divine power. For this reason, lions that are to be used for formal and traditional applications must always be consecrated or 'Awakened', this is particularly true if they are to be used for a Qi Men application. A lion that has not been consecrated might look the part, but it will not have the power that goes with it. It will be as effective as going to war carrying a toy machine gun.

The ritual that is undertaken to 'Awaken' the lion is called "*Kai Guang* 開光" which translates to "Opening of Light". The most important part of the ritual involves marking the lion with a calligraphy brush coated with cinnabar, a process that is called "*Dian Jing* 點睛". The brush is dotted along the lion at various points to imbue it with divine energy, most significantly the dot of the pupils is made which allows the lion to 'open its eyes' – thus allowing the light to come flooding in.

The ritual of consecration will be performed on a carefully chosen Day and Hour that will allow the lion to access the most auspicious and powerful energies. This choice will usually be made by consulting with a Chinese Almanac or a Qi Men chart. It is important to note, however, that the energy of the individual performing the ceremony will impact upon the energy of the Hour and it is important to make sure that there is not a clash. It is vital that the human and time-related energies are able to work in harmony with one another in order to achieve the best result. The ceremony will always be performed by an individual of some significant spiritual standing, who has been empowered with the ability to bring the divine into the beast and that person will need to have been selected before a day and time can be chosen.

The ceremony usually takes place in an open public space, often in front of a martial arts school. An area will be selected which will have a formal 'entrance', a central ceremonial area and a viewing area. At the centre of the ceremonial space, an altar will be prepared with an incense burner containing three small and three large sticks of incense flanked by two red candles, one on either side. The altar may be dedicated to *Guan Yin* 觀音, the Buddhist Goddess of Mercy, *Sun Wukong* 孫悟空 and *Guan Yu* 關羽 in which case an image of *Guan Yin* will be placed in the centre of the altar, with *Guan Yu* on the left Green Dragon side to represent peace and *Sun Wukong* on the right White Tiger side, representing warfare. It is important to note that different

醒獅

Newly consecrated lions paying their respects at the altar.

martial arts schools may choose to invoke different deities, some may choose only to invoke *Guan Yu* where others may choose one or more Daoist deities such as *Xuan Wu* 玄武, the God of Martial Arts. To the left hand side of the 'entrance' there will be flags and musical instruments, and to the right hand side there will be weapons: this follows the traditional Chinese concept of "civil left, military right (*wen zuo wu you* 文左武右)".

During the initial part of the consecration ceremony, the drums are played in a soft rolling rhythm accompanied by clashing cymbals and gong.

During the ceremony, the lion will be covered in a large square of red cloth and as we have previous stated, the body of the lion is only attached when the ceremony is just about to take place. The ceremony begins with the lion being placed in front of the altar, the incense is then lit and specific deities are invoked. In the case of Southern Lions, these deities will be related to the type and colour of the head. At this stage, speeches may be given by esteemed attendees such as public officials or other notable members of the community. It will be necessary to prepare three cups of wine, three cups of tea and sweets, fruits and cakes – these are given as offerings symbolising "three sets of three". The number three or "三", in Mandarin, sounds like the word "*Sheng* 生" which means to bring forth, produce or be given life.

At the zenith of the ceremony, as the master prepares to make the marks upon the lion, drums will be played softly in a rolling rhythm, cymbals will be clashed and a gong beaten. Traditionally it would have been dried pig's blood that would have been used to dot the lion but in the modern world, it is cinnabar powder mixed with water, referred to as (*Chen Sha* 辰砂), that is used. Alternatively, for the sake of convenience and because cinnabar is now thought to be toxic, red paint may be utilised instead. As the calligraphy brush is dipped into the red fluid, the master will recite the following incantation:

"*As the sun arises from the East, it bestows the brilliant light of spiritual virtues (Ri chu dong fan, wei wo ling guang* 日出東方, 唯我靈光)".

Regardless of the school that is performing the ceremony, this first line of incantation is always the same, following this, however, they may use an assortment of further incantations depending on their belief systems and desires. At this stage, a spiritual patron deity will be invoked. This spiritual patron deity will then bestow life upon the lion and the master will make the first dot which is always placed on the mirror in the centre of the lion's forehead: this opens the lion's third eye.

The mirror also serves the purpose of scaring away any evil spirits that approach, as they will be terrified by the horror of their own reflections. Next, it is the lion's eyes that are dotted, this opens the lion's physical eyes allowing it to see, and foresee, good and evil. After this, it is the nose and the inside of the mouth that are dotted, this allows the lion to draw breath. Dots are placed one by one on all the animal's limbs, all the way down to its tail and in this way, the lion is thought to very gradually come to life.

Once the lion has been completely dotted, it begins to move slowly, finding its balance and learning how to use its limbs as all newborns must do. As the lion gains in confidence, it becomes livelier and the music becomes louder. The lion itself will then pay homage to the deities that presided over its birth by bowing, first to the Green Dragon on the left, then to the White Tiger on the right and then finally to the centre of the altar. Lastly, the lion will perform *Cai Qing* 菜清 by eating the greens and spilling them in three directions.

If the ceremony is to follow traditional Daoist Qi Men practice, the first dance of the lion will act to bring the lion into connection with the Qi Men Ba Gua Formation. At the conclusion of this, the lion will exit through the Qi Men Dun Jia "Life Door" which will be infused with a special life force. It is at this stage that the lion will finally be thought to have become, not only alive, but fully 'Awakened'.

For example if the consecration ceremony is performed on 17 May, 2016 at 9 pm, the first dance of the lion will follow the route determined by the chart below. The lion will first enter through the "Open Door" which is located in the South sector where there is an auspicious formation. This will enhance the "awakening" process of the lion and also symbolically represents "*Kai Guang* 開光" or "Opening of Light". The lion will then follow a specific set of steps through the chart and then exit through the "Life Door" located at the West sector, thus giving "life" to the lion.

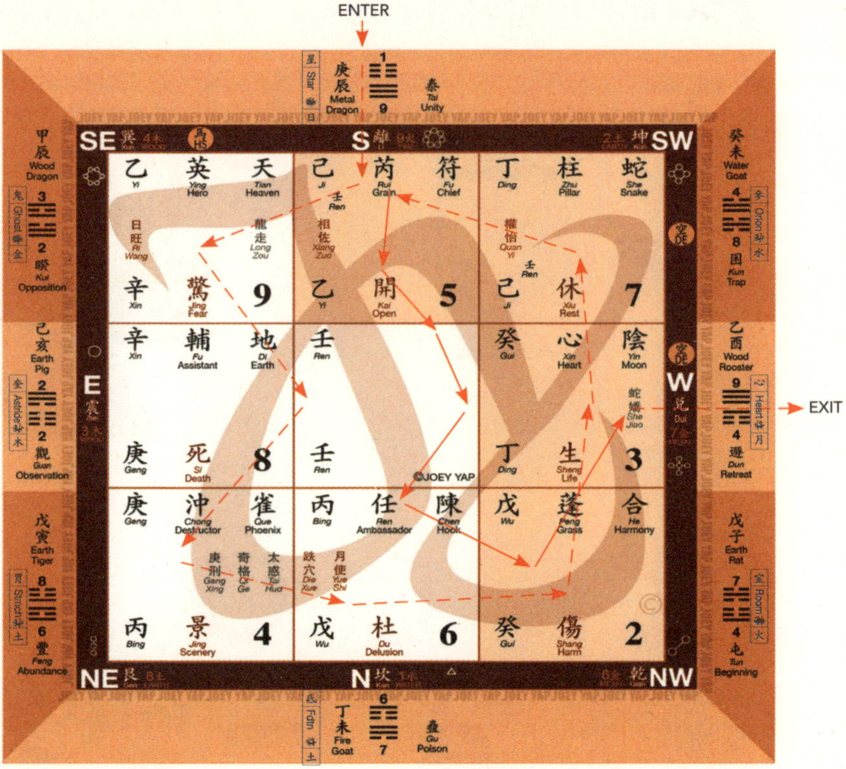

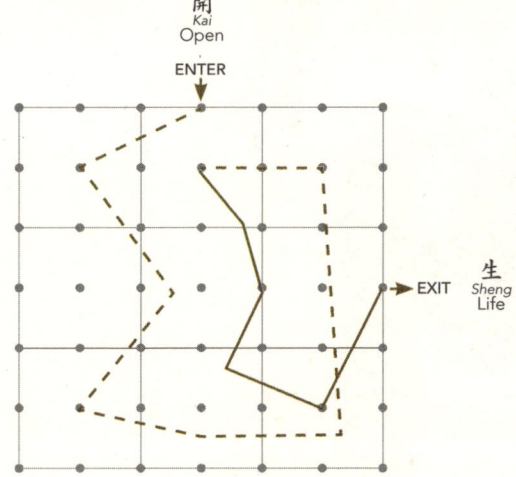

- - -   The dotted line indicates that the lion goes around one full circle, entering from the Open Door.

———   The solid line follows the Seven Stars Path where the lion exits through the Life Door.

AWAKENING THE LION

1.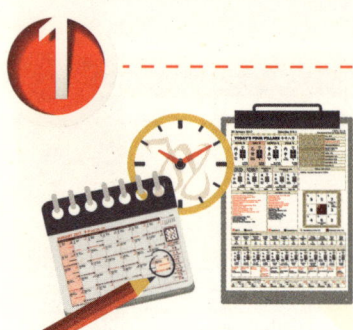
An auspicious day and time will be chosen for the consecration or *Kai Guang* 開光 ceremony.

2.
The new lion is laid out in front of the altar and covered with a red cloth.

9.
The lion then proceeds with the traditional Lion Dance routine.

8.
The newly 'awakened' lion then begins to perform for the first time by offering three bows. The lion will then perform *Cai Qing* 採青 by eating the greens and spilling them.

The Art of Lion Dance

Chapter 3

The Art of
Lion Dance

The Art of Lion Dance

A wide variety of skills and demonstration fall under the art of Lion Dance. These skills may range from a simple stance to highly complicated acrobatic stunts that require skilful coordination and lots of practice and training. However, before any Lion Dance performer starts leaping through the air in complicated and unique bounds and flips, there are common stunts and performance skills that every member of a martial arts school or Lion Dance troupe must be able to perform.

There are usually three to four parts that make up the Lion Dance: the head, the tail, the percussion team and the Laughing or Big-Headed Buddha, the latter of which is not always present in a performance. The percussion team normally includes instruments such as a drum, a gong and several pairs of cymbals. Everything works in sync during a performance to create the high-energy movements and rhythms of the Lion Dance.

The most recognisable position in a Lion Dance is the head. The performers who manipulate the head must be very versatile and very athletic. In order to play this position to the fullest, the performer must develop the skill to make lion-like movements using only their lower body. These movements include gestures like scratching oneself or trying to catch a ball. Meanwhile, their upper body is used to mimic the lion's head movements, which leaves the hands and arms free to control the finer details such as the lion's eyes, eyelids, mouth and ears.

醒獅

Lion Dance performers demonstrating their skills

The Art of Lion Dance

The performer who plays the lion's tail may often be overlooked by the casual observer but it is nevertheless an important and physically demanding role.

Meanwhile, the tail tends to be overlooked, since it is not as eye-catching and dynamic as the head and other parts of the troupe. Nonetheless, it plays an important role and it can be one of the hardest positions to play in a Lion Dance troupe. After all, it involves following every move of the head performer. However, keep in mind that this is not an easy position, since the tail performer is usually working with a limited field of vision!

The person manoeuvring that section of the lion costume has to work while bent double and crouched over, and so there is no visibility around him except the footwork of the head performer. He must also match both the steps of the head and the rhythm of the music. When performing stunts and acrobatic tricks, all these factors can make the tail performer, one of the most challenging positions compared to the others. This is even more challenging for the performers when the special Qi Men Dun Jia formations and steps are involved. Due to the additional ritualistic complexity and formality, it takes great precision, skill and agility to execute this flawlessly.

The role of the drummer tends to be played by the most senior member of the troupe. While many bystanders and laymen assume that the lion moves to the beat of the drum, it is actually the other way around. It is the drummer who follows the movements of the lion with his drumming and in turn, leads the rest of the percussion unit: the gong and the cymbals. If the lion makes a mistake, the drummer has to adjust the rhythm. The drummer tends to be the most senior member because they have to know the steps intimately and be prepared for any change in rhythm at a moment's notice, which requires a great amount of experience and versatility.

Of the entire troupe, the iconic Big-Headed Buddha (*Da Tou Fu* 大頭佛) is an optional role that is not always found in every performance. The Big-Headed Buddha is frequently a large full head mask that is at least twice the size of a normal human head, hence the name. This mask is usually painted pink if the character is the female Jade Green Willow (*Mi Ciu Niang* 咪翠娘). The performer wears a robe and carries a fan made of palm leaves. The role is to tease and play with the lion. They must lead the lion to the lettuce, which the lion must catch and "eat" for good fortune. It may sound simple but playing the Big-Headed Buddha is actually very demanding.

The performer must be very athletic to be able to perform all sorts of leaps and acrobatic feats. Cartwheels, jumps and various martial arts moves, all while wearing the giant mask! Meanwhile, the lion, depending on what mood it is portraying, will either play with the Big-Headed Buddha or chase, bite or kick at him. In special Qi Men formations, the Big-Headed Buddha takes lead to usher the lion into the formation and helps the lion accomplish the designated tasks within the formation. In complex formations, the help of a Big-Headed Buddha is much welcomed by the lion performers.

Martial Arts and Lion Dance

Most martial arts academies practice and perform the Lion Dance regardless of the type of school or discipline. This is because the Lion Dance serves as an extension of skill, where students can enhance their training and skills through performance. No matter how easy the performers may make it look, the Lion Dance is a demanding performance that is considered a test of endurance and skill, as well as a weight training program, since it involves moving around for extended periods of time while carrying the heavy mask and cloth body. Secondly, not only does Lion Dance is made available to the general public, it is also a way for martial arts schools to earn extra income, especially during festive periods such as the Chinese New Year.

The training models of Chinese martial arts schools focus on strength and flexibility rather than body building. This training model places emphasis on channelling force (*yun li* 運力) through movements of lifting, drawing up, pushing or pressing and expanding. Although stamina, endurance and fluidity of movement are also cultivated, there is a specific focus on the mastery of the body by way of controlled movements. The Lion Dance allows for development of all these qualities through training, and in the process, it also helps the troupe members gain control and mastery together, thus creating tighter bonds between them and allowing for gradual development of the synchronicity required in martial arts.

Most martial art academies double as training schools for lion dancing as it serves as an extension of the skill.

Martial arts training for the Lion Dance involve three major styles; the Stances, the Steps and the slightly advanced Movements, all of which the performers are expected to know well. The lions can already start channelling metaphysical powers at the level of Steps, but only if it is done right. Depending on the expression that the lion has to portray, all Stances, Steps and Movements will be further imbued with emotions and characters during the performance. The ultimate goal of the training is to prepare the lion to perform the auspicious and ever highly anticipated *Cai Qing* 採青 or "Pluck the Greens" feat in the performance, during which certain effects and specific energies are channelled.

Stances

Stances are essential to every Lion Dance performer. They create a strong foundation which helps to keep the performers steady when performing under the weight of the lion head and costume. Without a strong foundation in stances, it can be a challenge to hold the heavy load and dance at the same time without adverse effects on one's balance and movement.

Therefore, the greatest emphasis is put on stances which the performers have to practice regularly, even when they are not in training. Stances are the basic building blocks upon which the steps and movements for the rest of the performance are structured. There are six basic stances commonly taught by the majority of martial arts academies. Note: The performer's body must remain erect and upright while being very still on the ground.

Horse Stance
(*Si Ping Ma* 四平馬)

This is the most basic stance. To perform the Horse Stance, performers stand at shoulder-width apart with their feet flat to the ground and parallel to each other. The back must be kept straight with the arms extended and the hips squarely underneath oneself. The knees must be bent and kept apart between the ankles.

Horse Stance

Bow and Arrow Stance
(*Zi Wu Ma* 子午馬)

Another common stance frequently found in many other martial arts is the Bow and Arrow Stance. It is a strong, firm stance where the weight is distributed 60/40. The knee of the front leg is bent while the back leg is kept straight. The waist is fully turned facing forward, the knee and the foot of the back leg is turned in. Ideally the thigh of the front leg should be parallel to the floor.

Bow and Arrow Stance

Dragon Stance
(*Long Ma* 龍馬)

From the Horse Stance, the performer transitions into the Dragon Stance by first turning the head to the left. Keeping the back straight and the hips underneath himself, he would then step behind the left leg with his right. The arms are brought to the left as the performer steps into the posture.

Dragon Stance

White Crane Dipping into the Water Stance
(*Bai He Ta Shui Ma* 白鶴踏水馬) or
Cat Stance (*Mao Ma* 貓馬)

This is a flexible stance where most of the body weight is placed on the rear leg. The rear leg is bent at the knee and the weight is sunk straight down. The front leg is also bent at the knee with only the toes touching the floor. Ideally, both thighs should be parallel to the floor.

White Crane Dipping into the Water Stance

Low "T" Stance
(*Di Ding Ma* 低丁馬)

The Low T Stance is a combination of the Horse Stance and Bow and Arrow Stance. Both feet are placed parallel to each other on the ground and the performer faces the front. However, one leg is straightened out, and through this position, the performer is able to lower his body as far as possible, while combining upward and downward movements with both hands like the Horse Stance and then changing the direction to forward and outward movements like the second stance.

Low "T" Stance

High "T" Stance
(*Gao Ding Ma* 高丁馬)

For the High T Stance, the position assumed is similar to the Crane or Cat Stance. However, there is no tapping of the downwards pointing front, which remains stationary. The performer's body must be kept upright, with both hands held up to the chest but outwards, before panning from the extreme right to the left.

High "T" Stance

Steps

Once the foundational Stances have been mastered, the trainees move on to the second level, the Steps, which involve more footwork. The most essential qualities of these steps that must be mastered are jumping, friskiness, liveliness and the mimicry of a lion's movements. There are basically eight basic steps to follow.

Bow and Arrow Steps
(*Zi Wu Bu* 子午步)

These steps are executed in combination with the Bow and Arrow Stance, taking once step forward to the right and extending the arms up and outwards, then another step to the left and making the same hand movements. The Bow and Arrow is the basic step used in parades.

Two Character Yang Clipping Steps
(*Er Zi Qian Yang Bu* 二字鉗陽步)

The Horse Stance is first taken, with both hands near the chest. Then the hands are pushed upwards, the body is straightened and the feet come together, before the Horse Stance is assumed again. This is also known as Crab movement, since it requires sideways movements to advance.

Two Character Yang Clipping Steps

Unicorn Steps
(*Qi Lin Bu* 麒麟步)

Also known as Unicorn Stepping or Feminine Stepping since the legs are crossed to resemble the Chinese character for female, "*Nu* 女". The upper body is held in similar position to the Horse Stance, but the footwork involves the right foot crossing over the left foot with the knees slightly bent. The back leg is slightly extended with the heel up but does not completely leave the ground.

Unicorn Steps

Front-Back Eight Arrow Steps
(*Qian Hou Ba Jian Bu* 前後八箭步)

These steps are the forward and backward movements of the Bow and Arrow Stance. They involve taking forward and backwards steps with both hands extended forward and quickly pulling back in a retreating motion.

Three Stars Steps
(*San Xing Bu* 三星步)

These steps start with the Horse Stance. Both hands are first held to the right, with the body slightly turned but still facing forward. A short step is taken with the left foot crossing over the right, followed by the right foot moving out to the side to assume another Horse Stance.

Three Stars Scoop Beard Steps
(*San Xing Gou Xu Bu* 三星鉤鬚步)

A variation of the Three Stars Steps. The left foot does not cross over but is instead placed in front of the back foot which is slightly bent and supporting the weight of the body. Raising the pointed foot allows the body to rise, while the left foot sweeps over in an arch to brush the beard of the lion during the performance, and down onto the ground to assume the Horse Stance.

Left-Right Steps
(*Zuo You Du Li Bu* 左右獨立步)

These steps begin with a side stance with the feet slightly bent while keeping the performer's body erect and both hands raised high above the head. These steps allow for quick changes of position and are done facing either left or right. They are particularly used for switching performers.

Left-Right Steps

Seven Stars Steps (*Qi Xing Bu* 七星步)

A pattern of stepping with two basic variations performed according to the rhythmic patterns of drumming, is called Seven Stars Drum (*Qi Xing Gu* 鼓七星). It consists of various movements which are determined by the master depending on the purpose of the performance. In Qi Men, the Stars reflect the specific timing of an event and activity, and thus the Seven Stars Steps are some of the most useful steps used in Lion Dance performances utilising Qi Men methodologies.

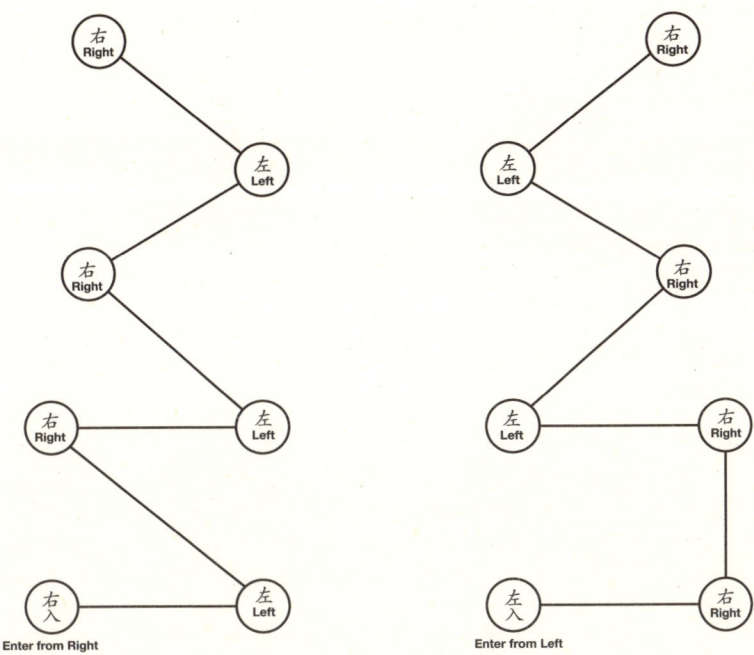

Seven Stars Steps in a Lion Dance performance.

There is a metaphysical Qi Men explanation for the presence of only seven steps in Seven Stars Steps. It is natural for every civilisation to always welcome auspicious energies and avoid the inauspicious ones. The steps in Seven Stars Steps are based entirely on this concept. In Qi Men, there are 8 Mystical Doors which appear randomly in all eight directions. Each door occupies a specific sector and they switch positions every 2 hours. The 8 Doors, when faced and channelled properly at specific moments of a Lion Dance performance, allow the performers to welcome their energies for helping the requester of the Lion Dance achieve his goals and objectives.

The channelling of the energies are rather simple. The requester would only need a paper with nine grids to map out the Doors' occupied sectors. He would then ask the Lion Dance troupe to begin the Seven Stars dancing steps at the sector where the Open Door resides and exit from the Life Door sector. There are only seven steps in the Seven Stars Steps because the performers would skip the Death Door sector.

The specifics of each Door can be found in the table below:

Doors	Auspicious for
開 Open	• New opportunities • The creation of new things • Overcoming all obstacles and challenges
休 Rest	• Recreational and happy activities • Nurturing relationships • Nobility and helpful people
生 Life	• Growth • One's livelihood and means of generating income • Influx and supply of things essential to progresses
傷 Harm	• Apprehending thieves and criminals • Collecting debt or money owed • Initiating a lawsuit against others
杜 Delusion	• Transmitting or delivering confidential documents • Avoiding negative mass media publicity • Escaping from a monotonous routine • Education and studies
景 Scenery	• Elections or any other grand occasions • Socialisation • Any form of engagement and favour seeking • Creating a good name or personal brand, goodwill and fame
驚 Fear	• Influencing others, creating pressure and fear on enemies • Warding or fending off others • Issuing a warning to enemies, negating their strength
死 Death	• Carrying out punishments • Burials and funerals • All worship, religious and spiritual matters

In view of these significances, the troupes would avoid the Death Door (unless they are dancing for funeral matters or if the requester specifically requested, which is very rare) because it is inauspicious, and execute their Seven Stars Steps in the shape of the Big Dipper Star.

Movements

After the first two stages of training, the performers are allowed to handle the lion head and will be taught various skills and techniques which are called the movements. These would include moving the lion's ears, winking or blinking, preening and licking, and other actions and poses.

These are some basic lion-like actions and poses frequently portrayed in a performance:

- The Lion Preens Its Legs (*Shi Yao Jiao* 獅咬腳)
- The Lion Scratches For Fleas (*Shi Yao Zao* 獅咬蚤)
- The Lion Dozes Off To Sleep (*Shi Shui Jiao* 獅睡覺)
- The Lion Playfully Rolls Over (*Shi Fan Shen* 獅翻身)
- The Lion Consumes The Greens (*Shi Yao Qing* 獅咬青)

In addition, various rules and courtesies required of the lion are taught in details such as:

- The Lion Receives Courtesies
  (*Shi Jie Li* 獅接禮)
- The Lion Gives Respects At The Temple
  (*Shi Bai Miao* 獅拜廟)
- The Lion Accords Courtesies At The Doorway
  (*Shi Bai Men* 獅拜門)
- The Lion Pays Courtesies Upon The Household
  (*Shi Deng Tang* 獅登堂)
- The Lion Respectfully Greets Other Lions
  (*Shuang Shi Hui* 雙獅會)

There are more advanced movements that use the basic legwork and stepping, which are also categorised under Movements. Unlike the previous movements, these are trained with the lion head and more specific instructions are given regarding their use and application in the Lion Dance. Some examples of such movements are listed below:

Exploratory Step (*Tan Bu* 探步)

This denotes suspicion and caution, and uses the Unicorn Steps as a base. It involves tip-toeing to reflect curiosity, carefulness and caution, and is used with the routine "Lion Emerging from the Cave *Shi Zi Chu Dong* 獅子出洞)".

The lions are performing the Exploratory Step with great caution.

Double Flying Step is usually used when the lion sees the lettuce.

Horse Riding Step (*Zuo Ma Bu* 坐馬步)

The Horse Stance is the basis of this movement which involves prostrating and showing obedience and humbleness. It is used when paying respect, receiving honours and in conjunction with ceremonial bowing and other courtesies.

Double Flying Step (*Shuang Fei Bu* 雙飛步)

This utilises a flying double-kick to express fright, surprise, lust or jubilation. Various speeds are used to express different emotions. It is usually used when the lion sees the lettuce (*Qing* 青).

Staying Horse Step (*Liu Ma Bu* 留馬步)

The lion takes a firm, stationary stance in either the Horse Stance or the Bow and Arrow Stance. It looks in both directions and behind, either moving the head on the spot or the performer stretches his arms forward and then snapping back. It involves further head movements such as nods, rolls and arches.

Staying Horse Step requires elaborated head movements.

Two-Pace Step (二字步)

Uses a variety of forward-moving stances, usually the Bow and Arrow Stance or the High-T Stance. It symbolises the lion's determination and resolve to move forward, and is thus portrayed with strong and definite stepping movements.

Quickhoof (*Diao Ti* 吊提)

This is used in conjunction with Tan Bu, but with jumps and acrobatic leaps as the lion advances and retreats. It adds expressions of slyness, mischievousness and avoidance.

Flash Steps (*Biao Bu* 標步)

Associated with the routine called "Lion Crossing the Bridge" (*Shi Zi Kuo Jiao* 獅子過橋), which involves quick manoeuvres and executions of the movements in this routine.

Pluck the Greens (*Cai Qing* 採青)

A unique skill and technique taught to the Cantonese Lion, it means "pluck the greens". It involves plucking a head of lettuce from a high place or an elevated platform. Depending on the difficulty, it may require various acrobatic leaps and balancing acts.

There are more advanced versions of these movements but due to their difficulty and creative complexity, they are commonly found only in competitive Lion Dance. However, depending on the skill and adventurousness of the troupe, these may sometimes show up in a normal Lion Dance session. These movements are referred to as the short skits, or the acts, called *Pai Chang* 排場.

Pluck the Greens is also known as Cai Qing.

Examples are as below:

- The Lion Ascending Heights
  (*Shi Zi Shang Tai* 獅子上台)

- The Lion Emerging From The Cave
  (*Shi Zi Chu Dong* 獅子出洞)

- The Lion Crossing The Bridge
  (*Shi Zi Guo Qiao* 獅子過橋)

- The Lion Crossing Over Mountains
  (*Shi Zi Guo San Shan* 獅子過三山)

- The Lion Makes His Appearance
  (*Shi Zi Chu Chang* 獅子出場)

Due to their complexity and the speed and dexterity required to perform some of these movements, Lion Dances can place a heavy demand on the athletic, acrobatic and martial arts skills of the performers. Both lion performers must be able to coordinate their movements for perfect harmony with each other. Due to established routines, most of the audience will be able to judge the quality of the performance. A martial arts school's reputation depends on the repertoire of *Pai Chang* that they can perform and teach.

Emotions of the Lion

There are usually 11 emotions which are commonly (but not absolutely) portrayed by the Lion to add more possibilities and diversities to the performance of the troupes.

These emotions usually include:

Emotions	Descriptions
Happy or Joyful	Mouth open, looking left and right, head raised, wagging the tail happily, to a rather fast music tempo.
Thinking	Stays put and stares at the objective before moving the lion head from side to side and up and down repeatedly as if examining a situation.
Suspicion or Caution	The cautious lion moves slowly, the head moving left to right, up and down and the drum plays soft and slow. The lion occasionally extends his leg to touch the object as if checking the object out.
Want or Desire	The lion reaches out at an object that it cannot reach.
Anger	Mouth closed, lion takes fierce strong quick steps with the head raised high and lowered quickly. The accompanying music is a loud drum with quick-short beats and occasional high drum. The lion raises the legs, wipes the beard and will knock things or someone down.
Scared	Lion body and head trembles.

Happy or Contented	Mouth open, but more subdued than overtly happy.
Drunk	Eyes get droopy, legs wobble as it goes left to right and back, stumbling forward and back, occasionally falling down, or falls rolling. While on the ground the lion tries to get up but falls straight back down, lion slowly goes to sleep.
Sleep	Eyes shut, sitting on the ground, the head sways slowly from side to side, drum beats getting slower and stops eventually. Malaysian teams tend to do it with a different beat. Drum taps, then gong (no cymbal) rim taps as if time ticking, gong as if time passes.
Alert or Wake Up or Startled	Jumps back up and blinks eyes.
Sad	Head lowered, on knees, soft drum, eyes partially closed, no gong or cymbals.

At this point of the training, the performers are said to be ready with the ability to combine various skillsets to execute their unique *Cai Qing* 採青 performance.

Did You Know?

Besides *Cai Qing* 採青 and other festive celebrations, the Lion Dance is also widely used in Chinese "white matters" which are funeral and burial matters. When the eldest or the most respected person of a household, organisation, or martial arts school passes, the White Filial Lion - *Ma Chao* 馬超獅 will be used to deliver a last grace to the respected.

The White Filial Lion is required because lions of other colours are considered the agents of Heaven once they have been awakened, and they are never allowed to be stained by the presence of death. When performing the funeral Lion Dance, the troupe members may choose to wear their uniforms instead of plain white shirts, but flags and banners would be excluded from the ceremony. The percussion ensemble plays slow and muffled drumming to express sorrow.

In addition, the lion head and the vehicle transporting the percussion ensemble is decorated with Banyan sprigs and branches. The Banyan (*Rong* 榕) is worshipped for long life and in funerals. It is symbolic of the phrase *Bai Nian Gui Shou* 百年歸壽, a literary and respectful statement for a good and easy death after the enjoyment of a long life.

When performing the dance, the performer bows down as low as they can and "kowtow" (叩頭) to the deceased. The lion will also make many other sympathetic gestures and expressions. One is to be a mourner in the performance of "Weeping Lion Before the Coffin (*Shi Zi Ku Ling* 獅子哭靈)".

For mourning and funeral matters, only the White Filial Lion or Ma Chao Lion is used.

Contrary to previous movements and patterns following Qi Men's 8 Mystical Doors, this time, the lion *would* start dancing from the sector of the Life Door that appears within the hour of the performance and exits through the Death Door, since this is considered an auspicious last trip for the deceased and the descendants shall be blessed with good virtues.

The ceremony is considered complete when the White Filial Lion is burnt after the Lion Dance. This denotes the lion's sending off and protecting the deceased's soul for a safe entry into the afterlife. In this ritual, the Seven Stars Path needs to be observed. The highest level of the Seven Stars determines the spiritual realm that the soul ascends to.

Music and Instruments

Chinese music was originally highly symbolic in character and is believed to be influenced by nature and the elements. The earliest known principle by which the Chinese classified musical instruments or sources of sound was according to the materials of which they were made. The choice of character was based on the connection of cosmological thought and ritual between these materials and the seasons, the winds, the harvest and by extension, human welfare, wealth and political power.

The Chinese divided their musical instruments into eight categories, corresponding to the *Ba Gua* 八卦 or Eight Trigrams. The eight musical categories, *Ba Yin* 八音, are as follows:

Jin 金	Metal instruments	Bell, gong, cymbals
Shi 石	Stone instruments	Stone chime
Si 絲	Silk or stringed instruments	Pipa/lute, harp, guzheng/zither
Zhu 竹	Bamboo instruments	Flute, pan pipes
Pao 匏	Gourd instruments	Reed organ
Ge 革	Skin or hide instruments	Drums, tambourine
Tu 土	Clay instruments	Ocarina
Mu 木	Wood instruments	Fish drum, clappers

There is a saying that goes, "Dancing is that by which one regulates the eight sources of sound and thereby conducts the eight winds" (*Wu Suo Yi Jie Ba Yin Er Xing Ba Feng* (舞所以節八音而行八風). As previously mentioned, the lion is accompanied by several instruments that at the very least include a drum, a gong, and a pair of cymbals. The drum represents the lion's voice or roar, and thus reflects its mood or emotion.

The drummer sets the tone for the lion, but ideally should the team be skilled enough, the drummer can and will follow the lion's lead. However, lest one thinks that the beats are random, there are set beats and patterns, of which the two most popular are the 7-Star and the 3-Star patterns. By playing at a fast tempo the players can invoke a mood that the lion is excited. Play it loud, and the lion seems angry. Play it soft, the lion is cautious and thoughtful. Playing it soft, low and slow and the lion is sad.

Dancing is that by which one regulates the eight sources of sound and thereby conducts the eight winds.

3

The Art of Lion Dance

Various types of traditional Chinese drums on display at the Drum Tower of Xi'an.

Drums

The drum is a very important part of Chinese culture. Its versatility means that it is used for military, civil and religious purposes as well as for musical reasons. There was confusion that drum skins were made of cowhide because the Chinese characters for ox and cow are the same. In the past, the skin was traditionally made from the hide of a water buffalo and coated with tung oil. Brass or iron nails hold the skin to the wooden frame. Bandings were used to keep the frame's shape and tightness of the drum while the same gauze-like paper used on modern lions is pasted over the wooden frame before it is painted. An enamel or lacquer coating over the very top helps contain the sound of the drum from leaking through the cracks. Also, to help fine-tune and prolong the resonance of the drums, tuning forks are located within the drum.

There are several types of drums used in the Lion Dance. They are:

Big Drum (*Da Gu* 大鼓)

In ancient times, these drums were used to strike the hours in tall drum towers. They were also used for rituals and for directing the movement of troops and other military manoeuvres. Because the sound of the Big Drum was sure to bring people out, together and in assembly, they were also called the Assembly Drum (*Tong Gu* 同鼓). The two-sided Big Drums are used extensively in the Northern Lion Dance.

Big Drums are commonly used in the Northern Lion Dance.

Flower Pot Shaped Drum (*Hua Pen Gu* 花盆鼓) or Jar Shaped Drum (*Gang Gu* 缸鼓)

This an elegant type of drum used for stage and indoor performances of the Northern Lion Dance. They are oddly-shaped with a large top which contracts to a smaller bottom. Both opened ends are covered with cow's hide.

Flower Pot Shaped Drum or Jar Shaped Drum are covered in cow's hide.

The Art of Lion Dance

Lion Dance Drum
(*Da Shi Gu* 大獅鼓)

The Lion Dance Drum is barrel-shaped but with an open mouth. It is used extensively for the Southern Lion Dance.

Traditionally, the drumming of Lion Dance is closely related to the mood and movements of the lion. However, the Malaysian Lion Dance performers have created a different kind of drumming by creating a tempo with which a lion's heartbeat and its body language can be mimicked. This gives the lions a heightened sense of intensity and liveliness.

醒獅

Lion Dance Drum gives the lions an increased sense of liveliness.

Cymbals

Cymbals

Cymbals are a metal percussion instrument which consists of two broad-rimmed circular alloy plates that are slightly convex so that only the edges touch when the two are struck together. In a Lion Dance, the most common cymbals used are made of very thin metal with turned-up rim and a characteristic central bell curve.

The usual way of playing the cymbals is to hold them vertically, clenched together. This way, the sound can be damped against the player's chest if necessary. They are usually struck together lightly, with a gliding movement. The sound is obtained not by clashing them against each other, but by rubbing their edges together with a sliding movement. They may also be played by striking them lightly with the edges or rims of the opposite.

Techniques for playing the cymbals:

• **Light Striking (*Qing Ji Yin* 輕擊音)**

Light clashing of the cymbals in an even tone which is used to denote a leisurely pace and movement. This is the most often used technique.

• **Heavy Striking (*Zhong Ji Yin* 重擊音)**

To show excitement, this is heavy clashing of the cymbals or working up and building to a crescendo. This technique is often used in conjunction with the first technique in the Lion Dance.

- **Grinding or Rubbing Strike (*Mo Jin Yin* 磨擊音)**

By sliding or gliding the cymbals together, a continuous muffled or droning sound is created. In the Lion Dance, this is most often used to denote a sleeping or sleepy lion.

- **Hitting or Beating Strike (*Pu Ji Yin* 撲擊音)**

This is done by either light or heavy clashing of the cymbals and then dampening the sound on the performer's chest. In the Lion Dance, it is used extensively in the 3-Star Drum and the 7-Star Drum.

- **Singular Strike (*Dan Ji Yin* 單擊音)**

This is either a soft strike of one cymbal with a stick or with the rim or edge of a second cymbal. In the Lion Dance, this is used when the lion is resting or slumbering on the ground.

Cymbals are played in a synchronised quick tempo with the drums in a Lion Dance performance. The Northern Lion Dance performances do not use the same types of cymbals as the Southern counterpart. The Northern Lion Dance cymbals are known as *Jing Bo* 京鈸, also popularly called the "Tibetan bowler hat". Northern Lion Dance instruments generally have different names, with the jing-prefix added to signify their Beijing origin. For example, their drums are known as *Jing Gu* 京鼓 and their gongs are known as *Jing Luo* 京鑼.

Gong

The Gong is made of a circular metal plaque. It is a sonorous percussion instrument that originated from Eastern China. It is usually played by the performer striking a headed stick at the centre of the plaque. Chinese Gongs are either flat and have their edges turned over, or have a turned-down rim and a central boss similar to Indonesia's *Gong Agong*.

Gong originated from Eastern China.

Techniques for striking the Gong:

- **Open Sound Strike (*Fang Yin Ji Fa* 放音擊法)**

An ordinary strike with the headed stick; it has a pause to allow the sound to complete without interruption.

- **Sound from the Bottom Edge (*Bian Yin Ji Fa* 邊音擊法)**

Downward and outward strike to the bottom edge of the gong which creates a different sound than the first technique.

- **Muffled Sound Strike (*Men Yin Ji Fa* 悶音擊法)**

Either of the first two techniques may be used, after which the hand is placed at the back side of the gong before striking the gong to create a dull sound. This sound may vary with the different ways the hands are placed on the gong's surface.

The Southern Lion Dance utilises a completely different type of gong called the Big Gong (*Da Luo* 大鑼) but more specifically called the High Edge Gong (*Gao Pian Luo* 高邊鑼). It is a heavy-hammered gong with high edges which resemble a high-rimmed baking pan. One of the most outstanding techniques of striking this type of gong is *Lian Chui* 連捶 which is a tolling strike to perpetuate the sound and also to regulate its tone and volume.

Supporting Characters in Lion Dance Troupes

Big-Headed Buddha (*Da Tou Fu* 大頭佛)

The Big-Headed Buddha serves as the comic relief and crowd controller in a Lion Dance performance. There are several legends regarding the origin of the Big-Headed Laughing Buddha. The first one is the *Nian* 年 Beast myth which also explains the origin of the lion, only in this tale the monk who tames the beast is replaced by the Buddha.

The other myth has it that the Big-Headed Buddha originated from a Monk Dance performer, *Li Jingdong. Li* was highly praised for his humorous depiction of the Big-Headed Buddha and ever since then, he was summoned to perform for many years, especially in the context of the Lion Dance.

A third, more contemporary myth tells of a lion who was looking for a mythical mushroom that was supposed to have great healing properties. In his travels he met a Buddhist monk who was also on a quest for the same mushroom. The two joined together to search for the mushroom. As they travelled together, the monk taught the lion Buddhism and in turn, the lion protected the monk from danger.

Normally, when the Big-Headed Buddha performs alongside the lion, the performers have to adhere to the drum's tempo as well as the lion's movements. Often, the movements of the Big-Headed Laughing Buddha are exaggerated. The performer of the Big-Headed Buddha holds a fan and is dressed in a monk's robe under the oversized Big-Headed Buddha head costume. It is to hide the performer's identity and real facial expressions from the audience.

The Big-Headed Buddha leads the lion in a Lion Dance performance.

Traditionally, each of the Big-Headed Buddha's movement has a fixed pattern and brings a specific meaning. It is the audience's obligation to try to understand each meaning of the movement in order to fully understand the performances. Examples of these movements are, sleeping, brushing teeth, waking up from sleep or vice versa. However, modern interpretations of the Big-Headed Laughing Buddha would often stray from the fixed patterns. The Big-Headed Buddha must lead the lion to the lettuce, which the lion would try to catch and eat, which denotes good luck. The lion, depending on its mood, will either play with, chase, bite, or kick the Buddha around, which is why the Buddha has to be quick and acrobatic.

Jade Green Willow (*Mi Ciu Niang* 咪翠娘)

There is a theory that the Big-Headed Buddha used to be a separate myth altogether but had somehow become confused with the character of the lion tamer monk. This myth spoke of the Big-Headed Buddha as a jovial and silly monk who lived in a temple with an ancient thousand-year-old willow tree. It is said that a spirit resided within the willow tree that could take on a female form known as Jade Green Willow. The spirit took a liking to the Big-Headed Buddha, and in an occasion when the rest of his brethren have went out, she appeared to him – openly flirting and playing with him.

A villager passing by overheard giggling voices and caught sight of the two over the wall. Amused by what he saw, the villager retold the story to others in an exaggerated fashion. The other villagers were equally amused by the tale, so they decided to turn it into a sort of comedic play during a festival and the story soon became a popular folktale.

The female character of Jade Green Willow occasionally appears alongside the Big-Headed Buddha in Lion Dance performances as a comedic foil, although it is no longer common nowadays. More often than not, the character appears in cultural performances as a female counterpart of the Big-Headed Buddha, although not many truly understand the story behind the character.

The Jade Green Willow usually appears alongside the Big-Headed Buddha in a performance.

God of Wealth is seen as a yearly symbol of prosperity.

God of Wealth (*Cai Shen* 財神)

In this contemporary era, the God of Wealth is commonly seen as a companion to the lions in Chinese New Year Lion Dance performances. However, the God of Wealth is not historically related to the Lion Dance and the partnership between the deity and the Lion Dance has only recently gained popularity. Yet people still tend to think of the association between the deity and the performance as historical.

This misconception is likely due to the fact that the God of Wealth and lions are both seen as a yearly symbol of prosperity to Chinese people especially during Chinese New Year. Lions are typically seen as the symbol of good luck, while the God of Wealth is seen as the symbol of one's increased fortune.

The Daoist Priest performs the rituals while the lions act as the protectors.

The Daoist Priest

For highly complex spiritual rituals involving the use of Lion Dance with Qi Men formations, the Daoist Priest wields the 7-Star Sword and performs the rituals while the lions act as the protectors. This type of dance rituals today is rare, and it is only found in ceremonial events held in old traditional temples.

Chapter 4

Lion Dance Traditions and Practices

Both the Lion Dance and the lion itself are more than just cultural symbols. The dance itself incorporates many mystical and ritualistic elements which is normally hidden behind what seem to the layperson as performance routines. In reality, many of these things are steeped in traditional rules, etiquettes and taboos. Every single gesture, observance and practice has significance and is done for a reason – whether it has its basis in ritual, ceremonial, traditional belief or even just plain proper manner and decorum. From a Chinese Metaphysical standpoint, certain practices and taboos are observed to enhance the efficacy of the ritual.

Over its long and colourful history, many ritual practices, taboos and traditional beliefs have been developed and these have been categorised as *Lion Dance Etiquette and Cultural Rules* (*Wu Shi Li Jie Yu Jin Ji* 舞獅禮節與禁忌). Bear in mind that since the Lion Dance is tightly intertwined with the world of martial arts – a highly proud, disciplined order with strict code of ethics – it should come as no surprise that the dance itself has also inherited many strict codes of conduct. Performers who behave out of line would not only reflect badly on the troupe but on their master or teacher as well.

According to common practice and tradition, and mostly because of traditional beliefs and fears, a strict adherence by all concerned would assure good fortune and the avoidance of accidents and injuries. From a metaphysical point of view, observing protocols and avoiding breaking traditional rules enable auspicious summoning processes to be carried out with a higher degree of accuracy. During specific rituals, especially during the Dotting and Awakening of the lion, this is of particular importance, since if the ritual or an incantation goes wrong, not only is it a bad omen, the lion head becomes useless and hours of work go to waste. Even when a lion has been properly Awakened, it needs to be treated with utmost respect by both the performers and the public, since at this stage it is technically considered to be a semi-divine inanimate being.

An altar set up prior to a Lion Dance performance.

One of the most iconic and well-known routines within a Lion Dance performance is *Cai Qing* 採青 or, "Pluck the Greens". From a traditional perspective, the *Cai Qing* steps have no strict protocols to follow or taboos to avoid, as long as the Awakening was done properly. However, since its key lies in its flexibility and customisability to suit the conditions and situations needed by the requester, it has a strong connection to Qi Men formations and the activation or destruction of such.

The general category or phrase used by martial artists concerning restrictions and taboo practices is "*Wu Shi Jin Ji* 舞獅禁忌", which literally means "*Spiritual Laws of Lion Dancing*". The various practices are based on traditional Chinese culture and traditions, as well as general Chinese traditional beliefs based on wordplay and symbolism. The traditional practices, etiquettes and spiritual laws found here are in no way definitive, but they are just some of the more common ones observed.

A new lion being consecrated.

Awakening the Lion (*Kai Guang* 開光)

Because the Awakening (*Kai Guang* 開光) is vital to give them their semi-divine power, lions without a proper Awakening should not be used for the Lion Dance. At best, any dance performed with an "un-Awakened" lion is futile and at worst, it can bring about misfortune.

In the initial Lion Dance performance after the Awakening ceremonies, the performers must carry a small bundle of green scallions and be given a red envelope to avoid any clash or mishap (*chong* 沖) from occurring.

Making offerings to the deities.

Before a Performance

Before leaving for any Lion Dance performances, obeisance with lighted incense must be made to the patron deity or guardian deity of the specific martial arts association. This is to avoid the possibility of any accidents or inauspicious events. Once the costumes and instruments for the performance have been set up, all percussion instruments must be silent until it begins. Most care must be taken to prevent the two drumsticks from clashing, as this is believed to bring about injuries and accidents among the performers.

When not in use, the lion costume must be properly placed and stored away. At no time should a person be allowed to step or jump over the lion. This is seen as putting oneself "higher" than the lion and is very disrespectful. The same goes before a performance when the lions are laid out in preparation for the performance. The troupe must make sure no audience members or small children step on or over the lion. No inauspicious or nonsensical chatter is permitted among the troupe members before any Lion Dance performance as well.

During a Performance

All references and mentions of injury, death, accident and the likes must be avoided in any conversations before and during a Lion Dance performance. When the performance is about to start, no other instruments should be heard before the first drum beat. This is because the drum is considered to be the lion's roar and leads the percussion ensemble.

When the lion enters or exits a household or building, it must not step on the threshold as this would bring bad luck and cause injuries to the members of the Lion Dance troupe. Performers must ensure they step over it when passing through a door. When exiting a temple, the lion may not turn around. Instead it must back out and exit rear end first. Performers wearing masks to lead or tease the lion such as the Big-Headed Laughing Buddha are not allowed to speak during the performance. This is a standing rule followed not only among Chinese Lion Dance troupes, but also the Japanese and Korean Lion Dance performers. To prevent the performer from accidently or inadvertently calling out, all masks have a horizontal bar or knob inside it for the performer to bite on, in order to hold it in place and to prevent him from opening his mouth to speak.

Some rules are simply common-sense principles that are adhered to for the safety of the performers. Should the lion be performing in a formation, and there happens to be a stray dog or cat running into the formation, all actions must stop to avoid the possibilities of injuries. A lion should also under no circumstances go under a clothes-line with hanging clothes to prevent the lion from getting tangled up in the clothes, thus causing injuries to the performer or possibly damaging the costume.

There are also some rules and taboos that came about during a time when lion dancing was far more competitive and aggressive, and when some performers were also involved in gangs. Back

A Lion Dance performance consisting of four lions at the entrance of an office building

then, while a Lion Dance troupe roamed the streets during a performance, the percussion members had to protect the drum from rival gangs. In extreme cases, the drummer also carried a knife for protection. Because the drummer drives and carries the rhythm of the performance with his drumming, it was vital that he was not interrupted or stopped in his performance.

Another rule that happens to be a holdover from that more competitive era is when two Senior Lions (*Lao Shi* 老獅) or *Cai Qing* Lions (*Cai Qing Shi* 採青獅) from different martial arts schools meet each other on the street. In such a case, no raising of the feet is allowed as this is seen as a sign of aggression. Usually, the master of each school will push each of their lion heads down while walking past the other lion. Raising the lion head in the presence of another lion from a different Kung Fu school is considered a sign of disrespect to the other school.

Bowing

Bowing before and after Lion Dance performances is considered good etiquette. It may not seem obvious to the unobservant eye, but a lion has different bows which portray different degrees of respect, as well as practical reasons. For instance, the Triple Bows of Great Homage (*San Xian Li* 三獻禮) is usually only reserved for temples or ancestral hall altars. The Honour Bow (*Bai Zun* 拜尊) is a general ceremonial bow used for Senior Lions or a lion used for the *Cai Qing* ceremony (as the vigorous movement of the bow is meant to depict the lion's energy and strength). The Ordinary Bow (*Xing Li* 行禮) is commonly used when the lion has to perform in a confined space.

There are protocols for bowing in various situations, places and occasions. When a lion passes a temple or shrine for example, it must respectfully acknowledge the deity by bowing; or when two friendly lions meet, they acknowledge each other through nodding bows without raising any feet (as that would be taken as a hostile gesture). The latter gesture is similarly accorded to stone lions guarding the doorways of certain establishments.

As an agent of Heaven, the lion does not bow to any living person except for an emperor, who in Chinese tradition is considered the Son of Heaven. While at times it may be observed bowing to a Head of State, the lion is in actuality acknowledging the leader's office instead of the person. Similarly, a lion does not actually accord any respect to the bride and bridegroom during wedding ceremonies when it bows, but rather to the Chinese character "*Xi* 囍" which represents the God of Happiness (*Xi Shen* 喜神).

Lions according respect by bowing.

Visitation Protocols

Being a frequent fixture at various celebrations and festivals, the Lion Dance is often required to be performed at different locations, ranging from temples to common households. Unsurprisingly, there are protocols to be observed at specific locations. Temple visitations in particular, are steeped in protocols. Despite its status as a divine being, the lion is not a deity and therefore, must show utmost respect and humility at such premises.

In short, it must not behave in a rowdy or impertinent manner and must accord respect to representations of mythical guardian beasts such as dragons and stone lions found at the entrance, before proceeding to offer the proper salutations to the deities in accordance to rank and protocol, starting with the Earth Deity (*Tu Di Shen* 土地神). It is required to enter the temple alone, left foot first through the right door, and never through the middle door. Traditionally, gifts would be presented to the lion after it has paid all the proper respects to the deities. The lion then exits through the left door, head lowered and backwards without turning its back.

Depending on the nature of the venue a lion visits, there are protocols which must be observed.

When visiting a household, the same protocols are observed at the entrance depending on what is found there. Normally, the lion would accord the necessary ceremonial bows at the entrance before proceeding to "lick" (*Tian* 舔) the top and both sides of the doorway. This action symbolically adds spiritual protection as well as bring good fortune to the household. The lion then pays its respect to the Landlord Deity (*Di Zu Shen* 地主神) upon entering the premises. If there is an altar within the household, it is also necessary for the lion to offer its respect to the deity (or deities) in the residence. Next, the lion would proceed to the middle of the parlour (*Zhong Tang* 中堂) and offer three bows to the wall facing the front of the house, as this is traditionally considered the main part of the home. The gesture of taking leave by retreating backwards is only done here, after which the lion can turn around and exit through the main entrance without turning round again to offer bows.

A lion "blessing" an office space.

Visitations to business premises are almost similar to that of households, except the lion will also symbolically "lick" the signboard or logo of the establishment to bring good fortune. Upon entering the premises, the lion as usual, offers its respect at any altars or deities in residence, particularly that of the God of Wealth (*Cai Shen* 财神). In the absence of such, the lion will normally hover around the cash register or counter, traditionally considered as the seat of the God of Wealth. There are some spiritual laws and restrictions which are observed by the instruments accompanying the Lion Dance, where cymbals and gongs are to remain outside as these are said to bring to mind a Chinese funeral. Drums especially are barred from the main halls of temples as the face is made from the hide of an animal.

Lions performing in front of a temple.

General Taboos

There are also some general taboos related to the handling of the lion and other props related to the Lion Dance. For one, the lion should not be handled by a woman during her menstrual period. There is a standing Chinese belief that women who are menstruating are unclean and may not touch or participate in anything religious. Pregnant women, called *Si Yan Po* 四眼婆, are also not allowed to touch any of the percussion instruments, weapons, or the lion head. Flags, banners and the entire percussion ensemble may not enter the main hall of temples. When a lion head is broken or has become too old to use, it must be properly disposed of by burning it with votive and incense papers, accompanied by the proper rites and ceremonies called *Song Shi* 送獅, or more formally as the Lion returning to Heaven (*Shi Zi Gui Tian* 獅子歸天).

There are also taboos concerning death. Anyone who has had a death in the family and has not completed the period of mourning may not participate in the Lion Dance in whatever capacity. Only the White Lion can be used for funerals, since white is the colour of death and mourning for the Chinese. The use of colourful lions, Lion Dance banners and flags at funerals are prohibited. Only the percussion instruments are allowed for such occasions.

Old and damaged lions must be properly disposed by burning them with votive and incense papers together with the proper rites and ceremonies.

Anyone who wishes to receive good luck or dispel negative energy can request the lion to do so.

Blessing the Audience

When the lion performs its blessing on the requester, it will hover around and encircle the person to "bless" the person or to cleanse the requester from bad Qi or negative energy. This is where the lion's horns and mirror come into play since these features are used to ward off evil energy. Anyone who also wishes to receive good luck or expels negative energy can request the lion to bless them with its presence. After the lion has "plucked" the greens, it will also shower the audience with shredded pieces of the green blessings.

When interacting with lions, the audience needs to be practical and respectful with their behaviour.

Audience Behaviour

The audience also has to adhere to rules and practices while watching a Lion Dance performance. Sometimes the lion will interact with the audience to make them feel more involved, especially when there are little children who may be excited or scared by the fierce expressions of the lions, including the loud drumming. Some people may also believe that by touching a lion, it will bring them good fortune. While there is nothing wrong with petting the lion's hair, such as the eyebrows, it is prohibited for people to touch a lion's horn or its mirror. This is because these two features are used to ward off evil energy, and touching them may bring bad luck to a person.

From a more practical and respectful perspective, people should not try to touch or smack the lion's body, back or hindquarters. This is because the body is basically a piece of cloth covering the performers, and by doing things such as spanking the lion, they are actually hitting, disturbing and disrupting the concentration of the performers.

Cai Qing is a flexible form of theatrical dance.

Pluck the Greens (*Cai Qing* 採青)

Pluck the Greens or *Cai Qing* 採青 is the ultimate skill that a performer can achieve within a martial arts school's long process of training in style and technique, accompanied and enhanced with music, props and costumes. The *Cai Qing* is therefore, a very flexible form of theatrical dance, consisting of a series of short acts, which may be choreographed into a complete story. Though this is not common knowledge to many, the requester can actually ask the Lion Dance troupe to dance a story that caters to his own situation, whether to break a Qi Men formation or to channel the positive energy of a Qi Men formation.

Traditionally, the practice of *Cai Qing* started with an old, popular custom practiced by the farmers of the Guangdong 廣東 province. Annually on New Year's Eve, instead of placing costly potted pine and cypress trees in front of their households like the wealthy folks did, the farmers would place a bunch of vegetables in front of their front doors.

This practice was called *Zhi Qing* 置青, and was meant as a prayer for good fortune and a request for blessings for their entire family. Another word for "*Qing* 青" is "*Lu* 綠", which also sounds like "*Lu* 祿", which means wealth and happiness. Wordplay aside, green is generally seen as the colour of lush growth, harvest and healthy crop.

As part of the performance during the Lion Dance, the lion will pick the *Qing* up and then tear it apart, before expelling it (*Pen Qing* 噴青) over everybody gathered at the scene. This is considered to be an auspicious sign. From this practice came the play of words "*Rui Qi Lin Men* 瑞氣臨門", which means "the auspicious Qi has descended over the household". As a token of gratitude to the Lion Dance troupes who brought the good luck to everybody, a red envelope (*Hong Bao* 紅包) is given to the troupes, hiding inside the greens.

During the Qing dynasty, the *Cai Qing* ritual was incorporated into the anti-Qing Ming loyalist revolutionary movement. When Lion Dances were held, martial artists involved in the revolution would pass information during performances by hiding it in the leaves of the *Qing*. The head dancer would cry out "*Cai Qing* 踩清", which meant "Depose the *Qing*" and was a play on the original *Cai Qing* 採青. This phrase was used as a signal to fellow revolutionaries in the crowd.

Aside from lettuce, other foods such as oranges, pomelos, tangerines, fish and crabs can be used in *Cai Qing*. While sometimes cabbages are used, the dense Chinese cabbage can sometimes pose a challenge to tear apart in a short period of time since it can be very hard. There are also three fruits that must not be used in *Cai Qing* at all. First is the pineapple. In Hokkien, the pineapple is pronounced "*Ong Lai* 黃梨" which sounds similar to "*Ong Lai* 旺來" which means "fortune comes". To split apart a pineapple would be incredibly inauspicious since it means destroying the requester's good fortune.

Then there's the apple, which in Mandarin is pronounced "*Ping Guo* 蘋果", with the "*ping*" sounding similar to the "*Ping* 平" which means "safety". Therefore, to tear up an apple means to tear up the familial security of the requester. Likewise, the symmetry of a pear and the seam that makes it look conjoined means that tearing it up also means splitting the requester's family apart. For these reasons, the pineapple, apple and pear should not be used in *Cai Qing*. White food should also not be fed to the lion, since white is the colour of death and mourning.

In a *Cai Qing* routine, chairs and tables used in the dance represent bridges or mountains, and buckets of water represent bodies of water such as streams, rivers, lakes, seas or oceans. The lion never just snatches the food and leaves. Each dance is an elaborate ritual that can be tailored to any situation the requester wanted addressed. For this reason, they must be arranged neatly even if they are not arranged in a particular formation. To leave them scattered and messy is a sign of disrespect to the troupe and the lion.

There are basically only two types of *Cai Qing*, which are called *Gao Qing* 高青 and involve greens placed in an elevated location, and *Di Qing* 地青, in which greens are placed on the ground. Depending on whether the requester is using the *Qing* to break or form formations, the possibilities can be endless.

Breaking a formation aims to break a person out of an unfavourable position. This could be a store owner suffering from overwhelming competition or a series of losses. A Lion Dance troupe performing a Lion Dance with Qi Men methodologies can break into the formation and bring the trapped person out of the metaphysical prison he was in. This is accomplished through a series of specific movements, organising the breakout itself at the right place and time based on the Qi Men chart, and using Qi Men tools such as the Eight Trigrams (*Ba Gua* 八卦).

Elevated Greens (*Gao Qing* 高青)

In the Elevated Greens or *Gao Qing* dances, the lion is usually required to recover the *Qing* (greens) that is placed at an elevated location. The *Qing* is usually attached to the crossbar of a bamboo suspended between two long bamboo poles. The lion will then scale one of the poles, or climb up a human pyramid made of the other members of the troupe. Alternatively, members of the troupe would hold up a round table with other members and a smaller round table on top to form a mountain. The lion then climbs the mountain to reach the food on top. This symbolises all the obstacles that the requester went through to achieve his goals.

Since *Gao Qing* scenarios utilise the narrative of overcoming a challenge, it is easy for a story or a specific formation to be shaped around the narrative to suit the situation faced by the requester. Through this Qing formation, all styles of Lion Dance can be ritualised into stories. While the Seven Stars Steps are pretty straightforward and direct, this is not the case for *Gao Qing* and *Di Qing*. There are at least three variations of styles for those who are considering to use *Gao Qing* as part of their Lion Dance.

1. *Qing Tian Zhu* 擎天柱, literally means "the pillar which bears the sky", another word for patriotic minister.

2. *Shang Die* 上碟, a homonym for "*Shang Die* 上牒" which means "to hand a memorial to the Emperor or Heaven".

3. *Shang Bo* 上膊, a homonym for "*Shang Bo* 上駁" which means "to register an argument or a contradiction".

Gao Qing dances are usually used to overcome challenges.

Qing Tian Zhu
擎天柱

For this formation, two poles are necessary: a tall sturdy pole with a short crossbar near the top and a long length of bamboo. Several strong men are needed to raise and brace the pole vertically. Only the performer with the lion head climbs up the pole, with the tail end being hoisted up with the long length of bamboo. When the lion reaches the top, he performs a stunt which involves wrapping his legs around the short crossbar right before *Cai Qing*. Once the greens are torn apart and scattered to the audience, the lion will unfurl a long congratulatory banner with phrases such as, "Good luck in the start of your business (*Sheng Yi Xing Long, Ji Xiang Ru Yi, Kai Gong Da Ji* 生意興隆，吉祥如意，開工大吉)", thus creating an exciting display.

醒獅

The lion is seen hurling congratulatory banner to the crowd.

Shang Die 上碟

Shang Die 上碟 requires the use of two round table tops and a long length of bamboo. The larger table is supported by ten persons and serves as the base. The other four men will hold up the smaller table in the middle of the larger table to support the lion as he ascends. The lion will only be controlled by one person and like in *Qing Tian Zhu*, the lion's body will be supported by the long bamboo. If the *Qing* is placed higher, the lion will climb onto the shoulders of another man to reach it.

Shang Die requires great skills and strengths from the performers.

Shang Bo 上膊

Shang Bo 上膊 which is also frequently known as the human pyramid (*Die Luo Han* 疊羅漢), is the toughest but most iconic formation among the three *Gao Qing*. It requires no props or equipment but relies on the strength of the entire troupe. Performers climb on the shoulders of other members who form the base of a pyramid, until they reach the elevated greens.

In *Gao Qing*, the *Qing* is frequently placed in an awkward position and at an elevated height to test the skills and abilities of the martial arts troupe, as well as to generate a sense of excitement for the audience. However, there are pros and cons to this. A Lion Dance performance is meant to bring auspicious luck and break bad formations, telling the triumphant story of the requester.

If the *Qing* is placed in a difficult position and the lion manages to retrieve it, this is considered a phenomenal success and the requester shall be able to overcome the deadlock. However, if the lion falls and injures itself during the performance, it is considered to be a bad omen, and also means that the obstacle could not be overcome. Other than providing a stunning performance, the highly *elevated Gao Qing* in a Lion Dance using Qi Men methodologies is meant to invoke the power of Nine Heavens.

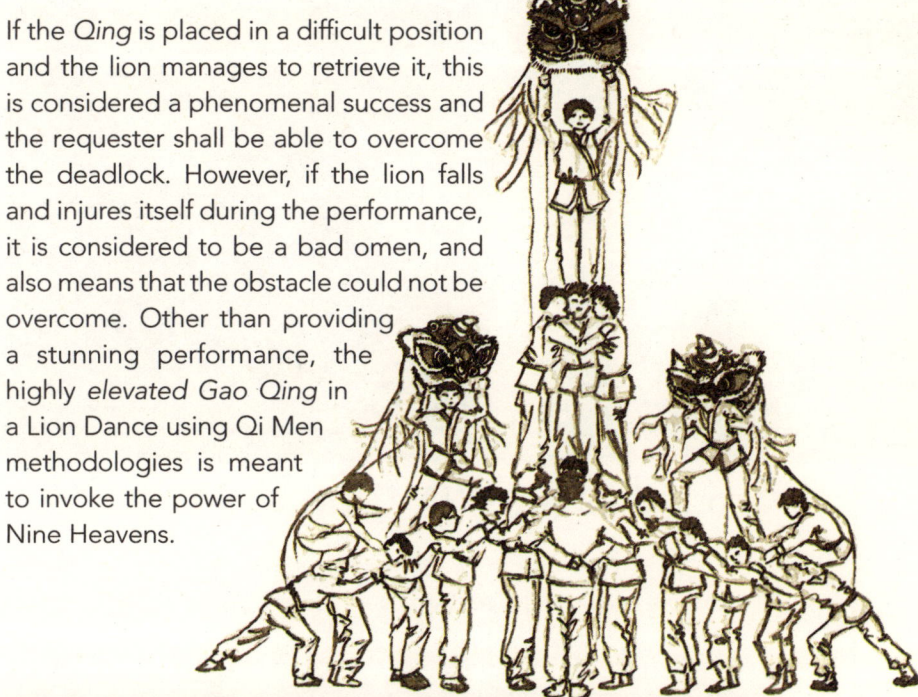

Shang Bo is where a human pyramid is formed.

In Di Qing dances, the lions must solve puzzles known as formation breaking.

Ground Greens (*Di Qing* 地青)

In the Ground Greens or *Di Qing* dances, the greens is placed on the ground in a specific pattern to form a puzzle that the lion must attempt to solve. Because it is performed on the ground, there are more possible outcomes to this dance. The puzzles can be based on animals, religion, word play, water, skill, literature, a Qi Men Dun Jia formation, or a combination of two or more of them.

In *Di Qing*, animal puzzles (formation breaking) are very famous. It narrates the story of the lion facing creatures (usually vermin) such as snakes, crabs, fishes, scorpions, centipedes and spiders. Usually the lion will have to dissect a representation of the animal formed from food, but occasionally a real crab or fish will be used. This in Qi Men represents the lion breaking the bad formation, overcoming the enemy and triumphing over evil, thus making for an exciting performance. On the other hand, *Di Qing* can also be very straightforward, with all the *Qing* placed together for the lion to eat and shower everybody with its luck.

There are plenty of variations to *Di Qing* formations. Some commonly performed *Di Qing* formations are listed below.

- Eight Trigrams Formation
 (*Ba Gua Zhen Qing* 八卦陣青)

- Year Formation
 (*Nian Qing* 年青)

- Venomous Snake Impeding Passage
 (*Du She Lan Lu Qing* 毒蛇攔路青)

- Crab Formation
 (*Xie Qing* 蟹青)

- Ever-Blossoming Flowers
 (*Si Ji Kai Hua Qing* 四季開花青)

- Treasure Under the Sea
 (*Hai Di Xun Bao Qing* 海底尋寶青)

Eight Trigrams Formation
(*Ba Gua Zhen Qing* 八卦陣青)

The Eight Trigrams Formation can be used for breaking a bad formation or calling upon the power of good Qi formation. That is the case of a single non-ritualised Lion Dance formation. However, when it comes to using it for Qi Men purposes, the entire floor plan of a person's house or property is considered to be the *Ba Gua* itself. This *Ba Gua* (floor plan) takes on the role of the Qi Men altar for energy summoning or breaking. Fret not, as a person is not required to set up a big Eight Trigrams as big as his house or draw big lines to denote the mark of the Trigrams.

The performance itself can be held in an open space in front of a person's house, such as the driveway. It is the *Ba Gua* that represents a person's house. A highly-skilled Lion Dance troupe can perform using the *Ba Gua* without any guidance, but in some cases, the sectors are demarcated with mandarin oranges or other items to denote the edges or angles. This is to ensure that the troupe performs the Lion Dance in the right sector, for to veer into the wrong one can be quite disastrous. It is in this *Ba Gua* itself, (i.e., a person's house), that this person will ritualise his own story into a Lion Dance performance and call upon its power.

Formation	Eight Trigrams Formation
Ingredients	Chopsticks to map the *Ba Gua*, mandarin oranges, lettuce and a red packet.

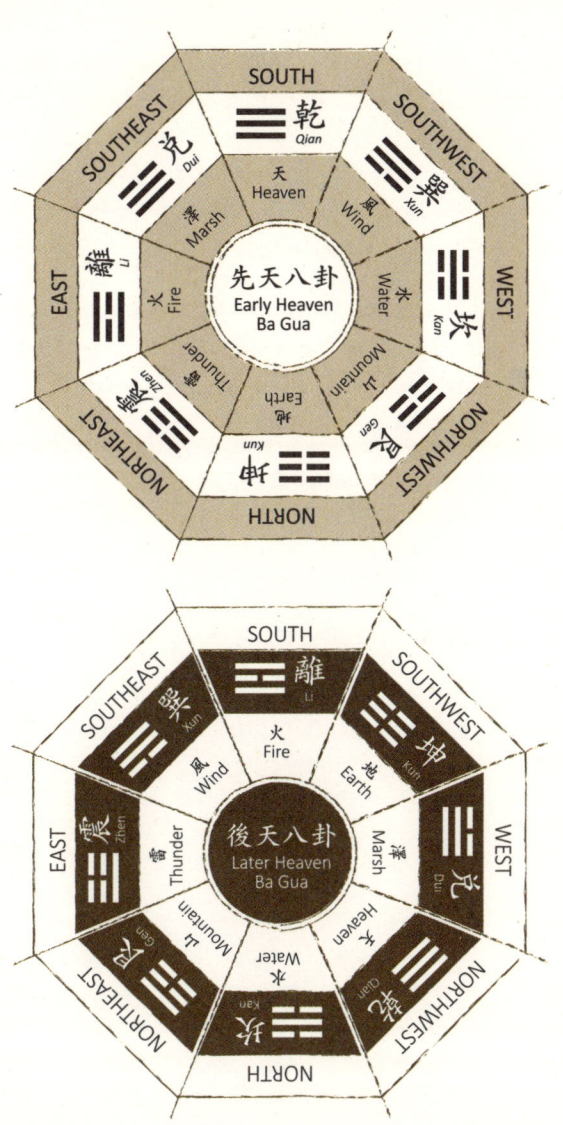

The Dance:

1. First, a series of broken lines will be drawn or mapped out using objects such as chopsticks on the ground to represent the Trigrams.

2. The greens will be placed at the centre. Then the step patterns of *Cai Ba Gua* 踩八卦 are used starting with the step pattern which starts by encircling in a counter-clockwise fashion at the bottom of the Eight Trigrams, the *Kun* 坤 symbol represented by a set of three pairs of broken lines and signifying Earth.

3. Then, the dancers proceed upwards and around the top of the Eight Trigrams, at the position of *Qian* 乾, with a set of three whole lines representing Heaven.

4. Finally, they move downwards again to the bottom right to the other trigram symbols.

Meaning of the Formation:

The Eight Trigrams Formation is the most important formation in a Lion Dance utilising Qi Men methodologies. It has many uses, since the essence of the Eight Trigrams Formation is about *Tai Ji* 太極, which can symbolise many things.

Year Formation
(*Nian Fen Qing Zhen* 年份青陣)

Also called the Lunar New Year Formation (*Xin Nian Kuai Le Cai Qing Zhen* 新年快樂採青陣). These New Year Formations are customised based on the Chinese zodiac calendar. The Lunar New Year Formation is meant to bring good luck to the requester, therefore its effects can only manifest fully if it is performed under an excellent or auspicious Qi Men chart. This formation is common because the time we use Lion Dances the most is during Chinese New Year whereby we sing our blessings and wishes during this time and hope for the effects to last the entire year.

Formation	Prosperous Monkey Year Formation (*Shen Xin Nian Kuai Le Zhen*申新年快樂陣)
Ingredients	15 chopsticks to form the word (*Shen* 申 – meaning "Monkey"), 12 mandarin oranges, lettuce, glutinous rice cake and a red packet.

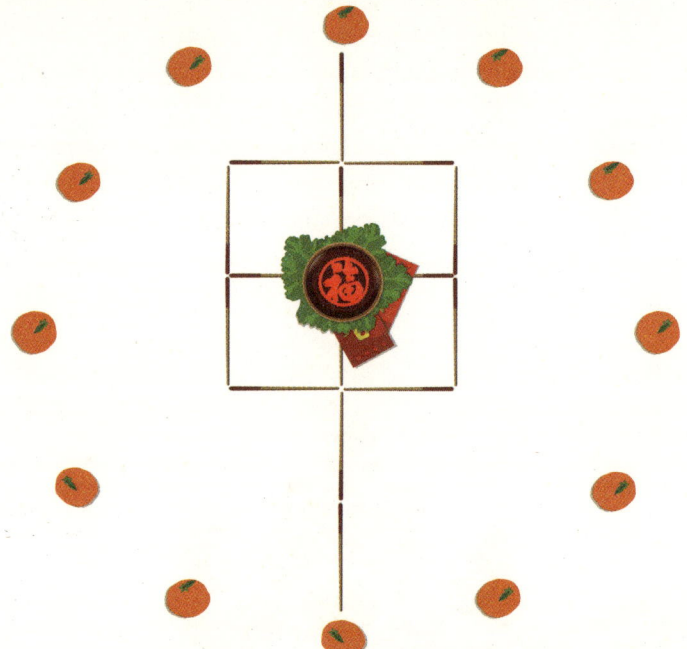

The Dance:

1. First the lion will curiously inspect the formation. Once it finds its curiosity satisfied, it removes the oranges. When the lion comes to the "*Shen* 申" character, it will inspect the formation again.

2. The lion will then take away all the chopsticks starting from the bottom and working its way to the top. This is followed by the rice cake, before it eats away at the lettuce stem. Then the lion will store the lettuce leaves, rice cake, and two mandarin oranges for later use.

3. The lion will reorganise nine chopsticks to form the character for Happiness (*Le* 樂) in simplified Chinese (*Le* 乐). It will then split the lettuce leaves and mandarin oranges to shower the audience with good luck.

4. After that, the lion will arrange the rest of the six chopsticks enclosing the character "*Le* 樂" to mark the conclusion of the dance.

5. After inspecting the final formation, the lion will pass the two mandarin oranges and the rice cake to the requester.

Meaning of the Formation:

Happy New Year! Gong Xi Fa Cai! May you have an auspicious year ahead and become better at everything. (*Xin Nian Kuai Le Gong Xi Fa Cai Ji Xiang Ru Yi Bu Bu Gao Sheng* 新年快樂 恭喜發財 吉祥如意 步步高升.)

Formation	Golden Chicken Calling the Spring Formation (*Jin Ji Huan Ri Zhen* 金雞喚日陣)
Ingredients	36 mandarin oranges, 12 sliced joints of sugar cane, lettuce, pomelo, red packet and a paper rooster.

*The Big-Headed Buddha is needed for this formation

The Dance:

1. Lay down all 36 oranges and 12 slices of sugar cane to form a shape that looks like the sun. Inside the oranges, place the pomelo and lettuce with a red envelope between the two. Stick the paper rooster on top of the pomelo.

2. The lion first inspects the formation. Next, it starts picking up the sugar canes and keeps them, before moving on to the mandarin oranges. The lion will then throw 24 mandarin oranges to the audience as he plays around with the crowd, while keeping 12 of the mandarin oranges to himself.

3. When the lion reaches the inner part, it will remove the paper rooster and pass it to the Big-Headed Buddha. Together, the two of them will play around for a bit. Then the lion will eat the pomelo and the lettuce before showering the lettuce at the crowd. As for the pomelo, the lion will slice it open into a flower and put it back in its original position. Then, the lion will place two sliced sugar canes next to the pomelo. It will slice another 12 oranges into flowers and use them to encircle the pomelo and sugar canes.

4. The lion will then use the rest of the 10 sugar canes to form the character "*Ri* 日" (*Ri* or Sun, or in this context, Spring) not too far away from the pomelo.

5. The Big-Headed Buddha will then join the performance with a big saucer plate. The saucer plate will be filled with candies and peanuts, which the Big-Headed Buddha will distribute to the audience as he goes around.

6. When the Big-Headed Buddha reaches the pomelo, he will pick up the pomelo, the 12 oranges and the 2 sugar cane sticks. He will then stick the paper rooster back onto the pomelo.

7. Along with the lion, both of them will give the greens back to the requester.

Meaning of the Formation:

Golden rooster calls to the sun, indicating that winter has passed and spring has come, step by step rising to the peak. (*Jin Ji Huan Ri Ying Xin Chun, Jie Jie Gao Sheng Man Tang Wang* 金雞喚日迎新春，節節高升滿堂旺.)

Formation	The Perfect Green Formation (*Shi Quan [Quan] Shi Mei Qing Zhen* 十全[犬]十美青陣)
Ingredients	10 mandarin oranges, chopsticks, a plate filled with pomelo, oranges, lettuce and red packets.

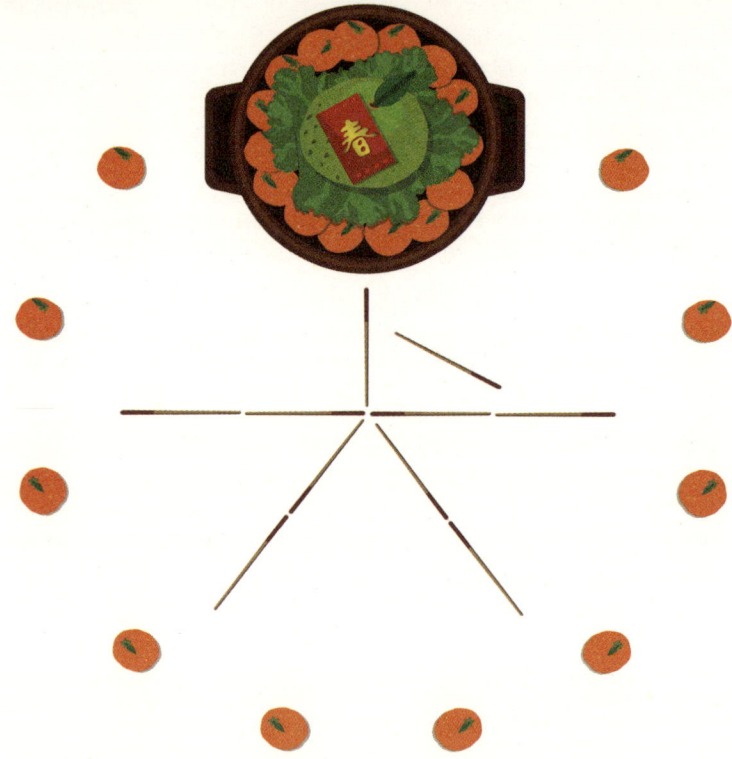

*The Big-Headed Buddha may assist in this formation

The Dance:

1. Set up 10 oranges in a circle and put one red envelope under each of the oranges. In the middle of this circle, put down a plate. Fill this plate with oranges and candies, one pomelo, the lettuce and a red packet. In front of the saucer, use around ten chopsticks to form the character "*Quan* 犬" (meaning "Dog").

2. The lion first inspects the formation. It then collects all ten oranges, and goes to the "*Quan* 犬" character and starts collecting the chopsticks from the bottom to the top.

3. When the lion reaches the saucer, it will distribute the oranges and candies to the crowd. It will then split the pomelo and the ten collected oranges earlier, into a flower and spray the lettuce over the public, while saving some for later use.

4. The pomelo is then placed back into the saucer and surrounded by the 10 oranges. The lion will eat up the last piece of lettuce and scatter into the saucer.

5. Not too far from the formation, the lion will use the collected chopsticks earlier to form the character "*Ji* 吉" and the rest of the oranges will be skinned to form the character "*Xiang* 祥", which, when put together, mean "auspicious". The lion will then surround the *Ji Xiang* 吉祥 with four "flower" oranges.

6. Together with the Lion, the Big-Headed Buddha will pick up the saucer and return it to the requester.

Meaning of the Formation:

Four seasons of fortune, auspicious all the way to the doorstep. (*Si Ji Ji Xiang Qing Xin Chun, Shi Quan Shi Mei Cai Yuan Dao* 四季吉祥慶新春、十全十美財源到.)

Venomous Snake Impeding Passage (*Du She Lan Lu Qing* 毒蛇攔路青)

The Snake Formation is popularly found in *Di Qing* patterns. It is used to represent an obstacle that prevents good fortune from entering a home or business.

Formation	Venomous Snake Impeding Passage
Ingredients	A spear, staff, three-sectional staff, chain or a stalk of sugar cane, lettuce, mandarin oranges, butterfly knives or similar weapons.

The Dance:

1. The snake is represented by a spear, staff, three-sectional staff, chain or a stalk of sugar cane as the body. The head is made from a lettuce, the eyes are oranges and the fangs are represented through butterfly knives or similar weapons.

2. The snake's head points towards the doorway and is placed on top of a red packet.

3. In a Qi Men formation, the fangs are in the sector with the Surging Snake and the greens should be placed in the Life Door sector.

4. The lion starts off by facing the snake head-to-head and then proceeds to investigate it, circling it in a clockwise direction.

5. Then, using fast and agile movements, the lion will try to gain an advantage over the snake. As it stalks its prey, it will display emotions as curiosity, fear, anger, happiness and cautiousness. It will jump over and around the snake, advancing, retreating and rolling as it attacks.

6. When it is ready, the lion will pounce on the snake's body from behind, pinning it in place. With the snake trapped, it will then blind it by removing its eyes, either rolling them through the doorway, or ripping them up and spitting them through the doorway.

7. With the snake blinded, the lion can then defang the snake. The snake can now be killed with little risk, and so the lion eats the snake, head first. The head is shredded and spat into the doorway, and after the body is eaten the lion goes to sleep.

8. Upon waking up the lion bows three times to pay respect, and the dance ends.

Meaning of the Formation:

The character for snake (*She* 蛇) is similar to the word for death (*Si* 死), so to remove the snake would be to remove whatever negative energy is killing the business or fortune.

Crab Formation (*Xie Qing* 蟹青)

The crab formation is another representation of an obstacle that prevents the entry of good fortune. Since the character for crab (*Xie* 蟹) sounds the same as the word for evil (*Xie* 邪), for the lion to eat the crab represents eating the evil that has been blocking the entry of good fortune.

Formation	Crab Formation
Ingredients	A bowl, pan or bucket (usually green, and never red like a cooked crab), chopsticks or bamboo, lettuce and mandarin oranges.

The Dance:

1. The crab is formed of a body, legs, claws and eyes. With a lettuce placed under a bowl, pan or bucket to make up the body, chopsticks or bamboo are used to represent the legs and claws, and oranges or tangerines are used for the eyes.

2. The lion starts the fight by facing the crab. Just like against the snake, the lion approaches the crab carefully. When it is ready to pounce, it will leap onto the crab from behind and pin down on its legs and claws.

3. The eyes are removed and rolled, or ripped up and spat, towards the business, home or the person of honour. The claws and legs are torn off and discarded. The lion head performer tosses the shell into the air with his feet and catches it in the lion's mouth.

4. The lion approaches the lettuce three times, and in the third approach, it will eat the lettuce, after getting hold of it. While it eats the lettuce, the lion performers will break up the chopsticks and use the pieces to form a message on the ground.

5. In another form of this dance, a large live crab is placed in a bucket of water with the mandarin oranges. The lion will stalk the real crab in the same way as before.

Meaning of the Formation:

This *Qing* is used disperse negative Qi from a person or property as it symbolises "*Shi Wu Po Xie (Xie)* 獅舞破邪 (蟹)" meaning "the lion dispersing the negative Qi". The crab (*Xie* 蟹) is used to represent "evil (*Xie* 邪)" as they both sound similar in Chinese.

Ever-Blossoming Flowers
(*Si Ji Kai Hua Qing* 四季開花青)

There are many variations to this setup. One such example uses objects that represent the five elements that also represent the five directions and the four seasons. A piece of Wood represents the East, Fire represents the South, Metal represents the West, Water represents the North, and a mound of dirt representing the Earth is placed in the middle of the formation. Buried under the dirt is a tangerine and the *Qing*, together with a red packet.

Formation	Ever-Blossoming Flowers
Ingredients	One large pomelo, four mandarin oranges, lettuce and a red packet.

The Dance:

1. A large pomelo is placed on the ground with a mandarin orange on each of the four corners. They represent the four directions, North, South, East, West, which in turn respectively represent Winter, Spring, Summer and Autumn.

2. A simpler alternative is to replace the pomelo with another mandarin orange and to simply scoop up each of them in the proper order. Each fruit is sectioned off into four pieces and the skin peeled off.

3. The lion then takes the pieces and forms a Chinese character such as "*Wang* 旺" (meaning "Prosperity") on the plate or floor after eating the lettuce.

4. The peels are expelled as the lion reawakens after its nap and the plate is then presented by the lion to the person that requested the Lion Dance.

Meaning of the Formation:

This *Qing* is used to bring auspicious luck to the requester as it symbolises "*Kai Hua Jie* Guo 開花結果", which means "prosperity and fruitful gains".

Treasure Under the Sea
(*Hai Di Xun Bao Qing* 海底尋寶青)

Formation	Treasure Under the Sea
Ingredients	A pan, silver coins, mandarin oranges, lettuce and a red packet.

The Dance:

1. A pan of water is placed on a low stool. Floating on top is a head of lettuce and a pair of mandarin oranges. Scattered on the bottom of the pan are silver coins.

2. The lion gathers the silver coins and takes a mouthful of water, before blowing it all out in a spray. The lion then removes the pan from the low stool, and while holding both the lettuce and the tangerines empties the water in front of the door.

3. After that, the lion, still holding the pan in its mouth, takes the head of lettuce and the pair of tangerines and presents them to the person who is responsible for setting up the formation.

Meaning of the Formation:

Mandarin oranges are called "*Kaat*" in Cantonese, which sounds similar to the word for good luck and auspiciousness in the same dialect. Pouring the water before the front door is called *Lin Men* 淋門. By combining these two actions or phrases, it turns into the expression "*Shuang Xi Lin Men* 雙喜臨門", which means "double happiness visits the household". The presentation of the lettuce head is called "*Sheng Cai Da Xian* 生財大獻" which represents great riches and wealth.

There are various type of Qi Men formations to be accessed through the use of these *Cai Qing* formations. Keep these types of Qing in mind when starting the next chapter, since they form the basis for various examples of Qi Men formations.

Chapter 5

Qi Men Methodologies in Lion Dance

Qi Men Strategic Execution

Qi Men Strategic Execution

Chapter 1 introduced the concept of Qi Men Dun Jia, the old Chinese metaphysical discipline that serves as a time and space energy mapping tool. It maps out the time continuum in four realms, which are Universe, Heaven, Earth and Man, while taking into account the eight geographical directions. Thanks to the detail that can go into a Qi Men reading, the right time and right place can be predicted down to the very hour, and so, one can isolate the exact moments in time when certain actions can be carried out to the greatest effect towards achieving the desired outcome.

The traditional purpose of the Qi Men method is to enable the practitioner to study the Qi Map for identifying an exact moment in time which offers the ideal conditions for an individual to take specific actions towards a specific outcome. This is where the Lion Dance with Qi Men methodologies comes in. The Lion Dance represents the specific action that needs to be undertaken to achieve whatever outcome one is seeking to achieve.

In the past, Qi Men was primarily used in military strategies to help leaders identify the exact time and place for advancing on their enemy, which would eventually clinch victory. This ability was invaluable to emperors and military strategists in avoiding ineffective strategy, poor deployment of military units and inaccurate assessment of the environment and surroundings.

In our 21st century society, to use a familiar metaphor, life for many can resemble a battlefield. With all the distraction on offer from modern technology and the pace of contemporary life, the pressure can be too much and its sources too numerous to mention. In the midst of such chaos, we are faced with a seemingly infinite number of decisions to make on a daily basis. Without guidance or assistance, we make them purely based on our limited experience, assessment and intuition. Some of those decisions may go well for us, while others could set us back in our path.

Qi Men Dun Jia is a tool that enables everyone to make those decisions with confidence rather than with just hope alone. Once the decisions are made, individuals can then press ahead with their actions with the knowledge that they are executing a plan that is inherently favourable to their hope of a desired outcome.

As noted above, the wrong decision may lead to a disaster. For example, a business decision that results in financial ruin, accepting a job that jeopardises our career progress or even marrying the wrong person that causes a family rift. On a personal level these decisions may only seem disastrous to us and a limited number of other people. Therefore, strategic execution is vital for coming up with a pre-planned action which would enable an individual to anticipate and engineer a desired outcome.

To understand which strategy to execute in order to achieve a desired outcome with Qi Men, an individual must select the chart that is most favourable to that particular execution. In order to select the right chart, they must first be able to read and interpret these charts.

Universe

Heaven

Earth

Man

Direction

There are in total 1080 Qi Men Charts, each with nine sectors and within each sector there are five components, which are Universe, Heaven, Earth, Man and Direction. The configuration of each of these components provides an indication of the specific date and time for an action which would produce the desired outcome.

Though at first glance they do not seem related, Qi Men has something in common with the Lion Dance. Both were once the exclusive purview of royalty and have only gradually entered the mainstream. The lions that inspired the dance were first presented as a tribute to the Han emperor. Elaborate Lion Dance performances were first staged in court for the viewing pleasure of royalty and officials. It is only after the art was introduced to the public when it became widespread and practiced to the extent of today.

Likewise, Qi Men follows a similar trajectory. In the beginning, this divinatory discipline was reserved only for the elite in society, specifically the emperor and members of the aristocracy involved in the military. This is because Qi Men was frequently used as a tool to plan military strategies and tactics, and so it was vital for that knowledge to only remain in the hands of the few. Because the knowledge of Qi Men was so restricted, it was commonly referred to as "The Emperor's Exclusive Imperial Knowledge".

Though both art forms may have been restricted in the past, today the Lion Dance and Qi Men have become far more accessible to anyone who chooses to explore and learn more about them. Significantly, Qi Men is the only surviving member of the three ancient Chinese metaphysical arts due to its many uses in forecasting and strategic execution. To this day, business magnates and political leaders have been using Qi Men charts to make crucial decisions on a daily or hourly basis.

In Chinese philosophy, the phrase "three teachings harmonious as one" (San Jiao He Yi 三教合一) refers to 儒 Confucianism, 道 Daoism and 释 Buddhism in a harmonious fusion.

Ritualising the Lion Dance with Qi Men

The influence of Chinese Metaphysics on the spiritual significance of the Lion Dance is not common knowledge. It can be traced historically to the Ming dynasty, during an era when the ritualistic side of the Lion Dance also included Daoist influence. It was also around this time when Buddhism slowly merged with Daoist philosophies and traditions. According to historical records such as the *Yongle Encyclopedia* (*Yong Le Da Dian* 永樂大典), many people practiced both religions as one, including several emperors such as *Yong Le* 永樂 (1403 – 1424) and *Cheng Hua* 成化 (1465 – 1487). In Chinese philosophy, the phrase "three teachings harmonious as one" (*San Jiao He Yi* 三教合一) refers to Confucianism, Daoism and Buddhism in a harmonious fusion, a philosophy that has been practiced for many years.

This was the era when various Daoist rituals became established and were introduced to the people, and the Lion Dance was one of their methods. There are various sects of Daoism but almost all of them utilise primarily time, space, events and matter – the Four Realms, the Five Elements and the Eight Directions (*Ba Gua* 八卦) in their ritualisation of the Lion Dance. It was around this time that Lion Dance formations were slowly integrated into festivals, events and celebrations.

Lion Dance formations cannot be put together in random. Not only do these formations require skilled martial artists, it takes a Daoist priest to devise the strategy for the Lion Dance movements. It is this integration of Daoist ritual and spiritual knowledge that makes the formations so important. It turns a skilled performance into a ritual dance which serves to unite Time, Space, Events and Matter in order to usher in positive Qi or to specifically negate bad energy.

Of course, Qi Men is no longer used for military matters. Nonetheless, it still has many uses, even if the battlefield setting has changed. After all, we still fight for recognition and advancement at work, and to raise the profile of our products and services against the competition. Managers and directors of companies face the same problems when it comes to orchestrating projects and motivating employees to perform beyond the benchmark. Above all, did we not place our hopes of achieving all these at the beginning of the year when we asked the Lion Dance to shower us with such luck?

The execution of all the above requires Qi Men strategies. Usually, the company may run a "Strengths, Weaknesses, Opportunities, Threats analysis" to take advantage of prevailing circumstances for driving their plans forward so that they would not fail. The application of Qi Men requires similarly detailed and meticulous calculation, and is used in order to identify the so-called "Golden Moment". The specific moment in a day is combined with an exact direction for a particular action to achieve the best outcome for a critical event. Historically, Chinese military leaders devised their best strategies and launched entire war campaigns solely on the basis of this method. Today, it is more likely to be applied by organisations to the creation of strategic marketing campaigns for product launches to achieve the maximum impact for their brands.

There are many ways of using Qi Men. Depending on what is needed, one can utilise the Qi Men charts to uncover the attributes of events that are happening at an instantaneous moment. It would go on to help one execute the correct strategies for achieving the desired outcomes. In recognition of Qi Men's capabilities, its function can be incorporated into the Lion Dance as part of Qi Men's Strategic Execution plan because:

- As explained in previous chapters, metaphysics, the Lion Dance and martial arts are intertwined in some way or other in the long history of ancient China. They are all based on *Yin* and *Yang*, the Five Elements and the Eight Trigrams, which are all the ultimate activators of time space events.

- This is a rare art form rarely practised in the modern era. Only a few martial arts academies transmit this knowledge to their students. Furthermore, only a few martial artists are also trained in Chinese Metaphysics. Additionally, not many Chinese Metaphysics practitioners recognise the Lion Dance as one of the tools of the trade since they regard it as more of a martial art form.

- Qi Men masters who know how to apply Qi Men in Lion Dance are usually found in Hong Kong, but even there they have become quite uncommon. This is because both the traditional Lion Dance (the full form that follows all the traditions) and Qi Men are considered rare arts, let alone exist together! This book is an attempt to keep this knowledge intact and pass it on to future generations, but it is by no means exhaustive.

The Art of Lion Dance

Lion Dancing, just like the Awakening of the Lion, should be performed on the right day, at the right time and in the right direction. For this reason the Lion Dance is part of Qi Men Strategic Execution, and requires detailed and meticulous calculation to identify the so-called "Golden Moment".

A thorough date and time selection helps identify the specific moment in a day, and when it is combined with an exact direction for a particular action, the best outcome for a critical event can be achieved. In today's Lion Dance, this is used for securing auspicious luck in health and wealth all year long, officiating martial arts schools or ceremonies, cleansing bad Qi, healing the Qi of a household, the creation of strategic marketing campaigns for new product launches, and many other important events.

Before venturing deeper into the combination of the Lion Dance and Qi Men Strategic Execution, keep in mind that there are a lot of possible styles that can be combined with Qi Men, and a person's imagination is the limit. However, to simplify things here are three basic Lion Dance moves that meet all Qi Men requirements.

Seven Stars Steps (*Qi Xing Bu* 七星步)

It is a pattern of steps which has two basic variations and performed according to a specific rhythmic drumming called 7-Star Drum (*Qi Xing Gu* 七星鼓). It consists of various movements to be determined by the master depending on the purpose of the performance. In Qi Men, the Stars reflect the specific timing of an event and activity, and thus the Seven Stars Steps is one of the most useful steps in a Lion Dance performance that utilises Qi Men.

Elevated Greens (*Gao Qing* 高青)

In a *Gao Qing* dance, the lion is required to retrieve greens that have been placed in an elevated location. The lion must scale a variety of poles, benches or human pyramids to pluck the greens. This symbolises the petitioner going through all obstacles to achieve his goals.

Ground Greens (*Di Qing* 地青)

In a *Di Qing* dance, the lion has to solve a puzzle in the form of greens laid out in a specific pattern on the ground. The puzzles can be based on animals, religion, word play, water, skill, literature or a combination of two or more categories.

Applying Qi Men to Lion Dance

When we execute our plan, it must be strategic so that it would yield the best results with minimal losses. By using the Qi Men Hour Charts (Structures) you can learn the type of strategy that will work for you and in which direction. Therefore, all you have to do is to follow the given forecast of that time. It is best to think of a Structure (*Ge* 格) as an option so that we can consider each Structure and look for the best outcome in a situation. Structures also help to identify the suitability of the situational circumstances to the intended decisions or plans.

You can refer to the **Qi Men Dun Jia 540 Yang Structure Charts** and the **Qi Men Dun Jia 540 Yin Structure Charts** for the Hour Chart that has been readily plotted for you.

All these books are available at The Joey Yap Store at
http://store.joeyyap.com.

Step 1 – Determine Your Objectives

In order to perform a Lion Dance using Qi Men Strategic Execution, you must first determine your objectives, which will be the main purpose of your Qi Men analysis. Are you currently seeking to break out of a formation to improve your current situation? Are you doing well and seek to do even better? Or better yet, are you seeking to break out and then prosper? Are you in a unique situation where you require special attention – such as cleansing or healing?

Now there are some exceptional cases in Lion Dances that utilise Qi Men. Let's say you intend to call on auspicious luck, but right after you have selected your auspicious Date and Hour, the Qi Men Hour Chart does not show any promising or auspicious Structures for you to execute your plan.

When you find yourself in this situation, chances are you need a formation-breaking Lion Dance rather than one that channels auspiciousness. You should not fret however, as this is not a sign of doom. It is however, a sign of putting an end to malicious luck before it even hits you. Since the Qi Men Hour Chart serves as a good personal forecasting tool, you should consider following the chart's Structures and execute your strategy accordingly.

Step 2 – Select Your Day and Plot the Hour Chart

All Lion Dances that use Qi Men Strategic Execution analyses are based on the Qi Men Hour Chart after selecting your auspicious day.

First of all, you must obtain the Hour Chart based on the hour of your reading. You can plot the Hour Chart by subscribing to our Joey Yap's QiMen 365 Professional Chart Plotter at

http://qmdj.masteryacademy.com/Account/Login.aspx

Step 3 – Superimpose and Analyse

Once you are in possession of your Chart, it must be superimposed on the "battleground" or the designated area for the ritual or dance to take place on the property. This location represents the building or property involved in the strategic execution. Prior to doing this, make sure to obtain the compass orientation of the location. The example in the next page, a Qi Men Chart has been superimposed over the driveway space. This is where the Lion Dance will be held, and so the sectors in this space must be surveyed carefully.

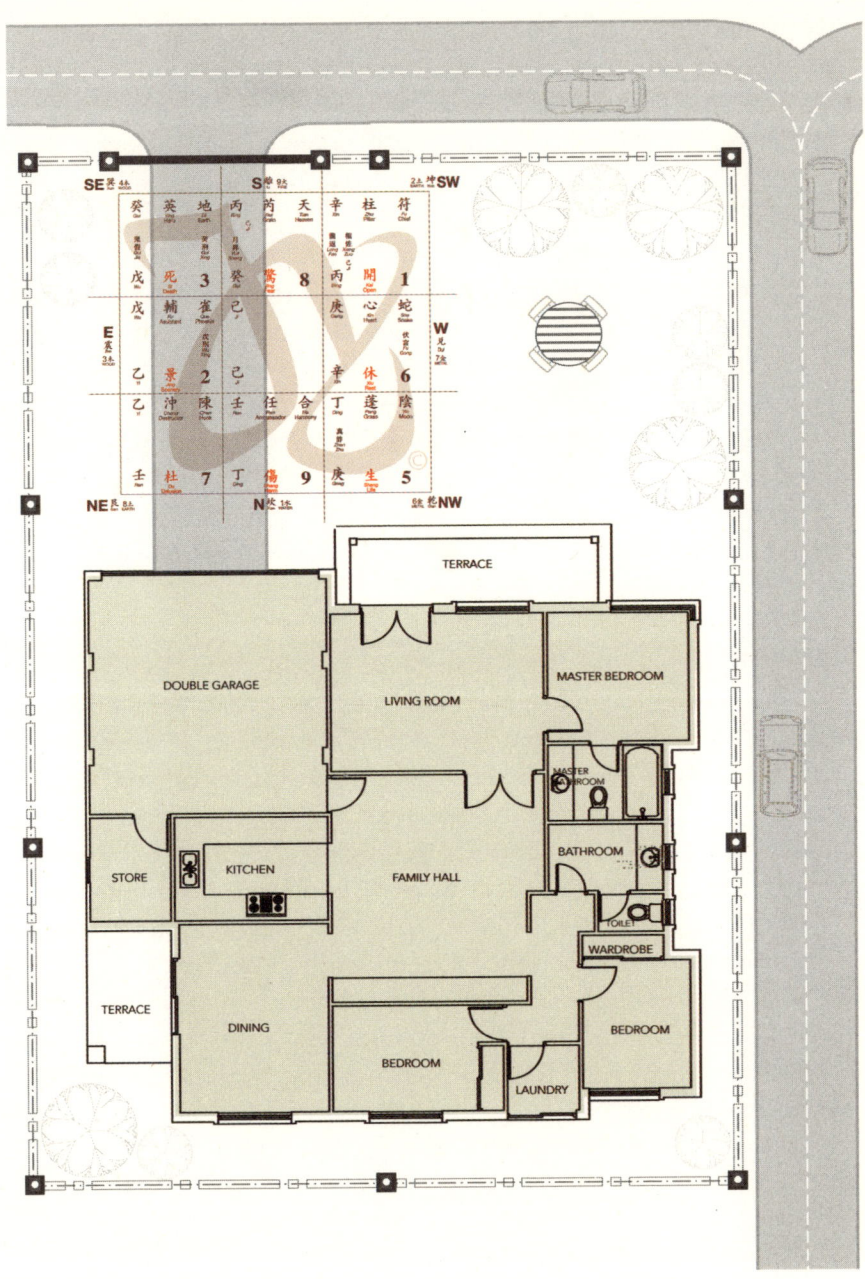

An example of a Qi Men Chart superimposed on a designated area for Lion Dance performance in an open space directly outside of a house.

Next, study the Qi Men Hour Chart and identify the sector you wish to analyse. Although there are a total of 1080 charts in Qi Men, for the Lion Dance the 24 common ones will do (12 auspicious Structures which require you to call upon its energy and 12 inauspicious Structures which require you to break out of it).

The most basic component that needs to be taken into consideration when plotting a Lion Dance formation based on your Hour Chart are the 8 Doors. The 8 Doors of Qi Men, also known as the Human Plate, represent the state of man and govern human actions. Tapping into the power of the 8 Doors means to maximise the potential of what we do in order to obtain the best possible results in life. Therefore, the goal is to activate the Door that has the power over the desired outcome, which is done through a formation. When the lion performs this formation, it activates the energies of the Door.

Similarly, when the petitioner finds himself in a bind and seemingly embroiled in chronic bad luck, the goal is to help him escape from it through the right door by "Breaking a Formation (*Po Zhen* 破陣)". However, his bonds must first be broken, and so the Door that ties him down (that he presently resides in) needs to be identified. Take for example the Harm Door, which may be causing him setbacks at work. By entering through the Harm Door and exiting via the Open Door, the lion leads him from his "prison" through the Open Door to freedom. In a case where someone just wishes to improve his current standing, the Life Door that represents his potential for growth is selected, as the entrance and the exit is the Door that "opens" potential opportunities for him.

The following table lists the 8 Doors of Qi Men, as well as the actions and events that they are suitable for.

The 8 Doors of Qi Men

Doors	Auspicious for
Open 開門	• New opportunities • The creation of new things • Overcoming all obstacles and challenges
Rest 休門	• Recreational and joyful activities • Nurturing relationships • Nobility and helpful people
Life 生門	• Growth • One's livelihood and means of generating income • Influx and supply of things essential for progress
Harm 傷門	• Apprehending thieves and criminals • Collecting debt or money owed • Initiating lawsuits against others
Delusion 杜門	• Transmitting or delivering confidential documents • Avoiding negative mass media publicity • Escaping from a monotonous routine • Education and studies
Scenery 景門	• Elections or any other grand occasions • Socialisation • Any form of engagement and favour-seeking • Creating a good name/personal brand, good will and fame
Fear 驚門	• Influencing others, putting pressure on and fear in enemies • Warding or fending off others • Issuing warnings to enemies, negating their strength
Death 死門	• Carrying out punishments • Burials and funerals • All worship, religious and spiritual matters

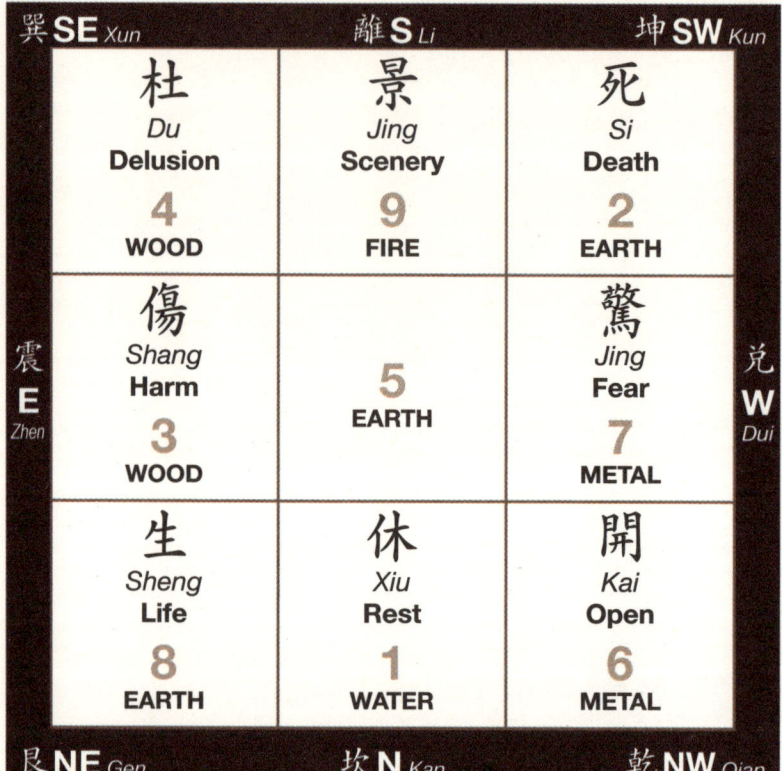

Each of the 8 Doors has a Natal Palace from which they begin their journey. The Doors rotate around the Eight Palaces every two hours, and are thus positioned differently based on the Day and Hour. The Doors exert different qualities in different stages as they move across the chart.

The Qi Men system is made up of several different components, such as the Deities, Stars, Stems and Doors. The Structures are identified through the Stem and their combinations that appear in the chart. Each combination results in a Structure that forecasts the result of the activity and indicates the possible outcome of an action which can be taken. They are formed by specific combinations of two or more components appearing together in the same Palace. They create synergy, where one component combines with one or more components to create a much greater sum than from just one individual component.

It is best to look at a Structure as an option, so that each Structure can be considered the best outcome of a situation. Structures also help identify whether the circumstances in that situation are suited to the intended decisions or plans. The following table lists some of the Structures that may appear in a Qi Men Chart. Some are very or moderately auspicious, which means that activating them through *Cai Qing* or the Seven Stars Steps will bring about good fortune. Others are less auspicious or even outright malicious, which means the breaking of formation is required to destroy negative influences.

24 Common Auspicious & Inauspicious Structures for Lion Dances

Highly Auspicious Structures

Lion Dance Strategy:
Formation Activation - Seven Stars Steps, *Gao Qing*, *Di Qing*

Name of Structure	Benefits
Green Dragon Returns 青龍返首	• Exceedingly positive formation, outstanding outcomes in all areas • Career progression is likely • Increased company profits for business owners • Quick resolutions of negative situations • Personal and professional relationships will flourish • Well-connected mentors will offer good advice • Working partnerships will be productive • Marriages will be happy and harmonious
Flying Bird Falls Into Cave 飛鳥跌穴	• One of the most desirable 10 Stem Combinations • An indication of very good fortune • Plans unfold without a hitch, success comes easily • Noble People will offer their help and support, particularly in career-based endeavours • Supports trade and investment, borrowing and lending money • Supports new projects and career development • Supports legal action • Personal relationships will improve • Travelling and moving will have good results
Jade Maiden Watching The Door 玉女守門	• Carries auspicious connotations in human relationships • Enhances the ability to form a strong affinity with others • Effects will be felt in personal relationships and friendships but may also have wider ramification in career development as well as educational pursuits • Supports development of good rapport with tutors • Positive for mediation and negotiation of disputes

Auspicious Structures

Lion Dance Strategy:
Formation Activation - Seven Stars Steps, *Gao Qing, Di Qing*

Name of Structure	Benefits
Dragon Dun 龍遁	• Often connected to big projects and important events • Supports new endeavours and developments, such as marriage and childbirth • Work-related travels are also likely to lead to an increase in wealth and profits • Has affinity to theological learning and the Element of Water (likely to be very successful)
Heavenly Dun 天遁	• Issues stability • Current levels of wealth and success are easily maintained • Sustains a comfortable life with few challenges • Supportive of retirement • Makes promotion a possibility • Suited to business deals and negotiations, property investments and making official announcements • Supports justice and judgement against transgressors
Wind Dun 風遁	• Supports publicity and all advertising and marketing ventures • Has positive effect on relationships, particularly marriages • May restore trust

Name of Structure	Benefits
Yi Noble Receives Envoy 日奇得使	• Ensures the right skill for the right job, thus supports most applications • Creates the opportunity to perform to the best of abilities • Opens doors to advisors and key decision makers • Makes it easier to obtain information needed for the job • Aids in pacifying aggressors, negotiating and closing deals • Suitable for beginning a new job or starting new businesses to great success • Gives positive indications for marriage
Yi Noble Rising Palace 日奇昇殿	• Has a particular affinity with knowledge • Often favours investigative endeavours and the securing of important and privileged information • Supports industrial and market research, creating positive ramifications for sales campaigns, marketing, business expansion and stock trades • Also has a positive effect on criminal investigations, especially with apprehending felons and bringing illegal acts to light • Promises auspicious outcomes for business-related travel, burial or funeral arrangements, moving houses and marriage
Double Deception 重詐	• Can make an individual appear more confident, powerful and capable • Rivals are likely to be driven to insecurity • If this person is careful, he or she may be able to secure a psychological victory long before the battle even begins • Beneficial for taking up a defensive posture and seeking information on the enemy • Supports self-improvement in terms of attitude, skills, education and even physical strength • Favours money-making endeavours and taking on new jobs • Supports those wishing to start a family and attempting to conceive

Name of Structure	Benefits
Heavenly Fake 天假	• Helps foster peace. • Beneficial to one who wishes to rid oneself of a run of bad luck • Positive for those who are taking examinations and advancing careers • Suitable to making plans and winning support for your endeavours • Can aid in winning the confidence of the people in elections, giving this person everything needed to achieve a victory
Ghost Fake 鬼假	• Helps those who need to rediscover themselves, find their focus and rid themselves of negative thoughts or intentions • Helps them find calmness and pacify the anger at themselves as well as others • Soon they will find themselves better equipped to offer help and support to others
Star Prosperity 星旺	• This person's financial fortunes may well take a turn for the better • They can find opportunities to turn their dreams into reality • Opportunities and new platforms will open up, signifying the beginning of many great things ahead • Their luck will definitely take a turn for the better

Inauspicious Structures

Lion Dance Strategy:
Formation Breaking (*Po Zhen* 破陣) - *Di Qing*

Name of Structure	Implications
Chief Ascending Structure 符勃格	• Indicates negative outcomes for major activities • This person may feel stabbed in the back or that some powers have been working against him • There is treachery afoot and this person may feel betrayed
Ferocious White Tiger 白虎猖狂	• There may be trouble ahead and a situation may become rather volatile • Avoid taking any significant actions or making any important decisions • This person is likely to be feeling rather anxious and uncertain; it would be wise to go with his instincts and stay his hand • Marriage, construction and important business negotiations may all end badly
Day Structure 日格	• This formation suggests misfortune • It would be wise to postpone one's plans and wait for more auspicious luck • Problems will arise and lead to lost opportunities
Hidden Stem Structure 伏干格	• Prone to careless approaches, failing to take into account all factors and overlooking important details
Big Structure 大格	• Causes one to not have everything one needs to move plans forward; it may be due to lack of support or missing logistical elements • There will be significant setbacks to overcome even if one's goals can still be achieved
Flying Palace Structure 天乙飛宮格	• Something outside of one's control will throw plans into disarray • Be prepared to rethink your entire strategy • This formation is unfortunate for both the Host and the Guest

Malevolently Inauspicious Structures

Lion Dance Strategy:
Formation Breaking (*Po Zhen* 破陣) - *Di Qing*

Name of Structure	Implications
Sitting Palace Structure 天乙伏宮格	• Represents a change or a loss of faith or support • A lack of cohesion and shared vision is likely to leave this person rather vulnerable and uncertain as to what action to take • This person needs to be prepared to defend himself
Heavenly Net Four Spreads 天網四張	• This Hour will fare more favourably for the Guest but not so much for the Host • Instead of initiating an attack, it is better to retreat and strengthen the defence • This Structure is one of the most inauspicious hours for executing something important and is an inauspicious direction to proceed in
Earthly Net Shelter 地網遮蔽	• This person will be subjected to corporate espionage or someone leaking confidential information • This person may be fed false information or have his plans become known to the enemy. • This person should rethink his strategy and keep all important plans to himself at this point
Tangling Snake 騰蛇妖嬌	• Indicates drawn out conflicts and protracted arguments • There may be no easy resolution to any battle and it would be exceedingly unwise to become involved in any kind of legal wrangle
Green Dragon Escapes 青龍逃走	• This formation is mistrustful of change and it offers no support to important decisions and significant actions • Better to rest easy • There is a risk of financial losses and derailed plans

Name of Structure	Implications
Mistaken Hidden Mode 伏錯休囚	• This formation indicates stagnation • This person will feel stuck in a rut and unable to advance his or her plans • Be wary of any expressions of frustration and impatience • This formation also indicates that feelings are being buried, leading to emotional stagnation which is equally unhealthy
Red Phoenix Diving Water 朱雀投江	• There will be frayed tempers around • Disagreements and discords are likely and some may erupt into lawsuits and legal battles • There are few auspicious outcomes indicated in this formation

Reminder: It is essential that you read the analysis provided before forming your own judgment about the forecast.

Step 4 – A Step Further: Customisation & Ritualisation of the Story

Other than the White Lion, each coloured Lion has specific abilities and usage. At the customisation stage, decide what type of lion fulfils your objectives. Is the *Guan Yu* Lion 關羽獅 needed to rouse your business? Do you want a *Zhang Fei* 張飛獅 or W*Zhao Yun* 趙雲獅 Battle Lion to help you fight off competitors? Or do you just want the stability that a *Huang Zhong* Lion 黃忠獅 can provide you with? Usually only two lions are used in a Lion Dance, even in a huge event where more than two lions are involved.

Some companies may want the entire array of lions present, but when it comes to the performance, the two most relevant to the situation will perform the *Cai Qing* 採青, while the other lions remain as supporting acts. The act can be shared between the lions, or if the performance contains more than one act, such as *Di Qing* 地青 and *Gao Qing* 高青, the acts can be split equally between the two lions.

You may recall from Chapter 1 that the props and ingredients used in formations can be switched out for another option, as long as they can be ritualised into a story. For example, if you intend to break the Heavenly Net Four Spreads Structure, instead of using the Crab or Snake formation, you could use a papier-mâché bowl and place the mandarin oranges in it. As long as they have the same significance, the Lion Dance will still work. The point of customisation is to relate the formation as closely to you and your situation as possible, so that the ritualised story makes more sense and applies to only you.

If you have insufficient space for your Lion Dance to perform *Cai Qing* (for example, dancing inside an office space), you can resort to using only the Seven Stars Steps without a formation and to let the lion manoeuvre around and help you call upon the same effect. Of course if you have a bigger office space, you can always perform *Cai Qing* in there with all the props set up.

We have provided four different scenarios and examples for your reference. These detailed examples in the next few pages will help you understand the process better.

Examples

Example 1: Improving a Business

John has been running his own Fast Moving Consumer Goods (FMCG) business for some time and he is very successful at it. In the upcoming Chinese New Year, he wishes to have a Lion Dance performance at his company to bring more wealth and success to his business. After checking his personal auspicious date, he proceeds to look for an auspicious Qi Men Hour, which he finds to be at 3.00pm on 10 January 2016 because at that time, the Structures are the most favourable.

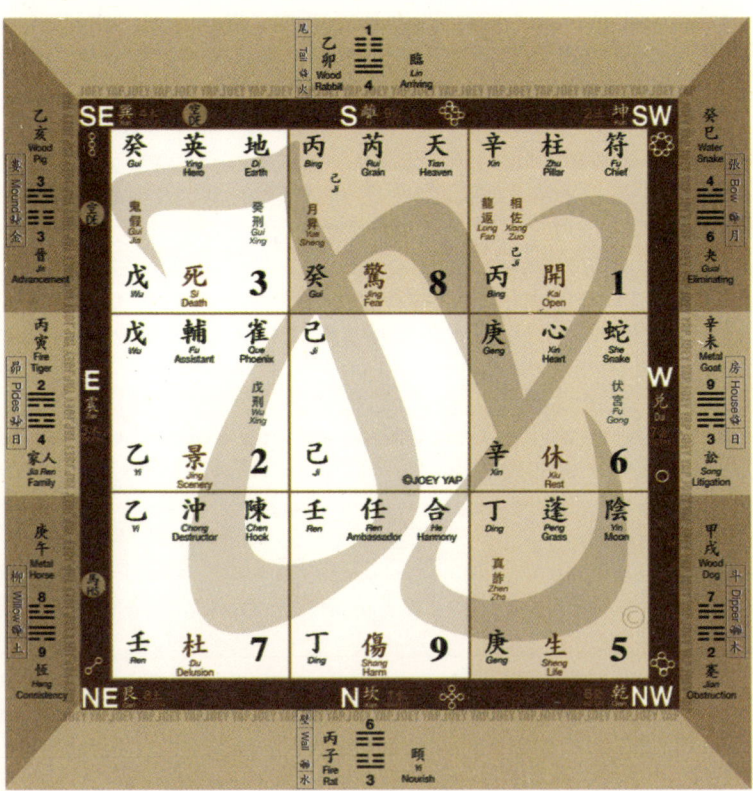

John's Chart 1

Since the entrance and the exit affect the outcome of the ritual, the very first step is to make sure that good Structures and deities occur at both good Doors. Since each deity and Structure combination can only occur once in a chart, John must also make sure that the good deity or Structure never falls into the Death Door.

The chart John has is a very auspicious chart. First and foremost, we can see that one of the most auspicious Structures, the Green Dragon Returns (*Qing Long Fan Shou* 青龍返首) occurs at Open Door, and that specific door is also blessed by a 7-Star Chief in the Southwest sector. Therefore, when the lion exits the Open Door, John will be "opening" his business to all manners of opportunities and good fortune.

Similarly, though not as powerful, the Life Door is also blessed with the good Structure, Real Deception (*Zhen Zha* 真詐) formed by the combination of the *Ding* 丁 Stem and the Life Door, making it an ideal sector for the lion to enter. Since John's case is considered a normal business case and there is nothing too specific to pay attention to, he can choose the lion of *Guan Yu*, *Zhang Fei* or *Zhao Yun* because any of these lions can rouse his battle spirit and raise business morale.

John's main goal is to improve his business, and since he is not facing any particular challenges in his work, there is no need for him to break any of the negative Structures in the chart. What he should prioritise instead is activating the energies of the right Qi Men Door with the help of the Lion Dance. This is done so in order for him to launch his career and business further ahead. For that purpose alone, he should choose the Open Door as an exit point, seeing that it has the ability to "open" new opportunities for him.

This chart is further empowered by the Chief Deity which has the ability to protect him from any negative Qi. With this auspicious combination in place in the Southwest sector, John should plan for the lion to perform *Cai Qing* or the Seven Stars Steps there to activate the energies of the sector.

Example 2: A Lion Dance in a Small Space

John wants to hold a Lion Dance in his home. He wishes to seal the deal with an important client, and for that he wants the Lion Dance troupe he has hired to perform *Gao Qing*. However, his house is quite small so it would be impossible for him to organise a performance in the living room or even in the driveway. So how should he plan for the performance?

John uses a different Qi Men Hour Chart for this scenario. In order for John to sign this deal and further his business success, he should activate the sector with the Nine Heaven (*Jiu Tian* 九天) Deity. The best way to activate this deity is to use *Gao Qing*. Since this performance requires a lot of space, it is best for him to have it performed outside the house. Therefore, the boundaries of the *Ba Gua*, drawn to represent the "battleground", and the performance of *Gao Qing* will both take place outside the house.

This performance will start off similar to that in Example 1. The lion enters through the Life Door in the Northwest Sector, where the Chief is also located. It uses the Seven Stars Steps as it crosses that sector. Then it exits the *Ba Gua* and enters the house through the Main Door once, bringing along the powers of the Chief to bless the house. Inside the house, the lion wanders from room to room (if there is a home altar set up, the Host can also choose to have the lion worship briefly in front of the altar). The lion then exits the house and re-enters the *Ba Gua* through the same sector (Northwest) it exited earlier.

For the second half of the performance, using the Seven Stars Steps, the lion then heads over to the sector with the Nine Heavens Deity, which is the West sector. Once there, the lion will perform *Gao Qing* as planned, scaling whatever raised props that are set up. The lion plucks the greens from the elevated position and blesses the host and audience with the shredded greens. Not only does this ritual activate the energies of the Nine Heavens, it gives John the power he needs to seal the deal with his clients and fulfil his ambitions. It can also help him break any negative Structures in that sector which may be influencing his actions.

The lion then concludes the dance by moving into the Southwest sector where the Open Door is located. By exiting from that sector, the lion activates the energies of the Open Door. Through this ritual, he "opens" his business to new opportunities which includes the deal he hopes to sign with his new clients.

Should John have a large enough space from the get-go to accommodate *Gao Qing* within the Ba Gua, the lion would not have to exit. However, for those with limited space, this is an option that they can settle for.

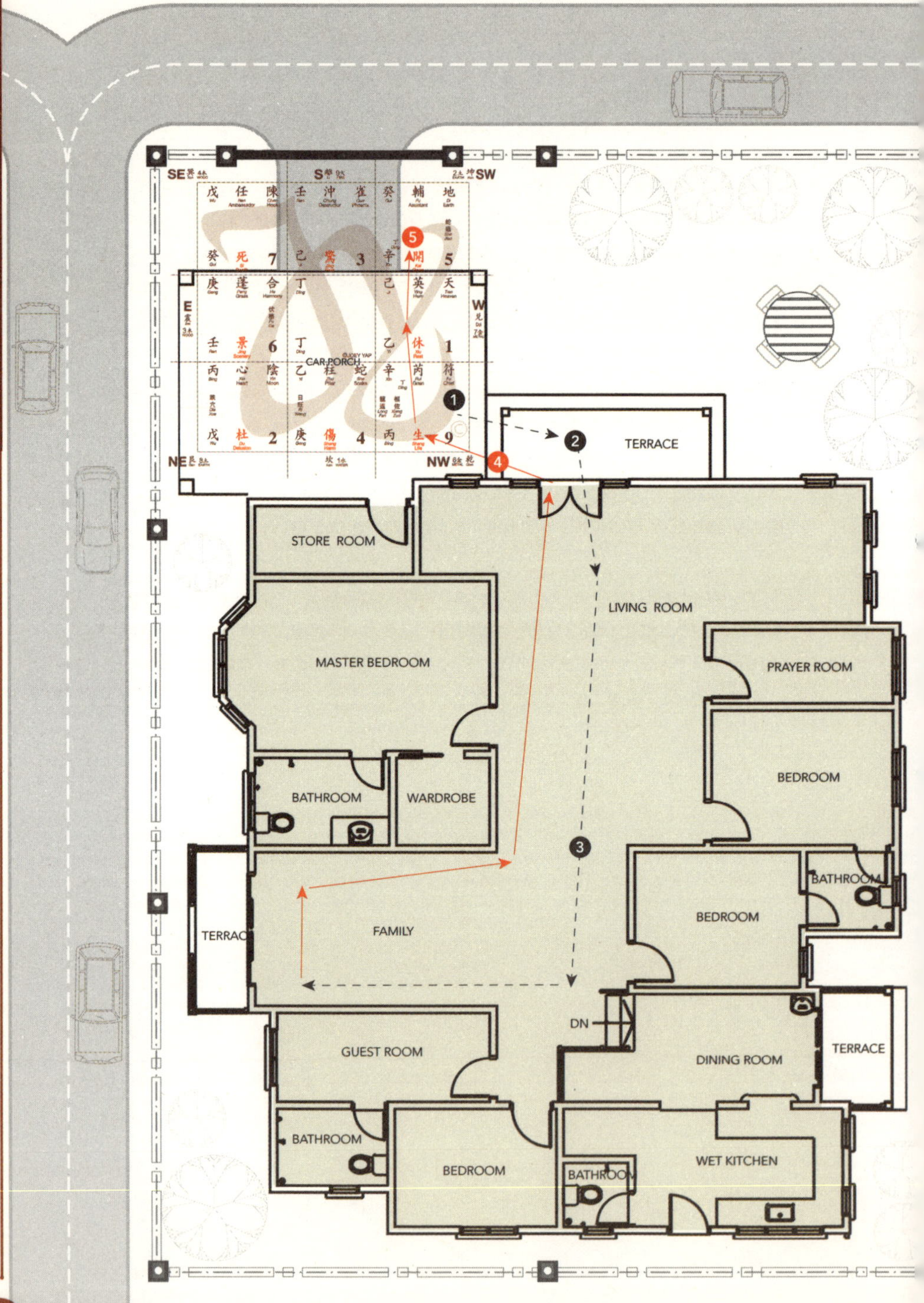

The Art of Lion Dance

John's Chart & House Plan

Example 3: Escaping a Dire Situation

Due to its negative traits and connotations, the Death Door is usually avoided in a Lion Dance with Qi Men. However, sometimes its energies can also be put to use, though usually only under dire situations. For example, John is not as well off as in previous examples, and in fact he is facing several dire situations like feeling unwell for a long time and he cannot seem to recover, his business is declining, his business partner is breaking up his shares, his family is falling apart due to his business woes, and this further deteriorates his overall health and mental well-being.

It is fair to say that the John we are dealing with today is barely hanging on and needs the cleansing of the Lion Dance. Assuming the same chart as Example 1 and the setup of at least one formation, John will need to guide the lion in a different Lion Dance sequence. This time, the entry point of the lion is the sector where the Death Door resides, while the exit point is the Life Door. He can choose to put two formations at both of these sectors if the situation allows. In this case, John can choose the *Zhang Fei* Lion since its tough and scrappy nature is best-suited to helping John fight the tough times ahead.

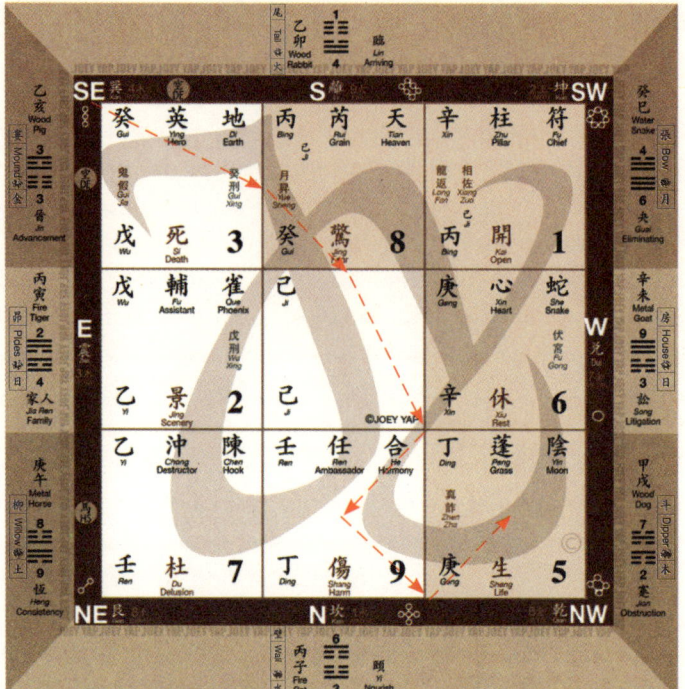

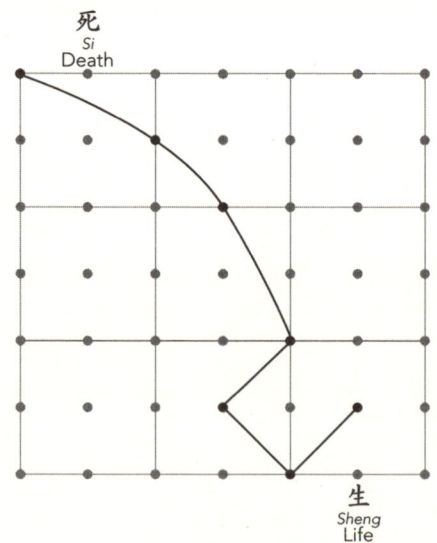

John's Chart 2

Instead of going through every sector and every door, John can choose to have the Lion Dance only at the Southeast and Northwest sectors because the goal is to fully channel all the energies at the Life Door, instead of having all the Doors scattering the energies away.

John himself can stand in the Northwest Sector (Life Door) and wait for the lion to arrive from the Southeast sector. When the lion arrives, it will encircle John to drive the bad Qi from him. If there is a formation at this Life Door sector, the lion can first attempt the formation before encircling John to syphon away all the bad Qi from him. The lion will then exit the Life Door sector, taking away all of John's bad Qi, thus bringing him back to "Life".

Example 4: Getting Married

What if this time John is getting married instead? Yes, a Lion Dance with Qi Men is applicable here as well.

For marriage, two lions are used. In this context John can choose modern lions instead of the traditional ones because marriage is supposed to be something exciting and happy, and so the pugilistic traditional lions are not required. For example, if John likes the colour of red, he could ask the troupe for a red lion and if his wife likes the colour of purple, he could ask the troupe for a purple lion instead (with longer eyelashes to indicate a female lion).

For marriage, the lions must exit the Rest Door since this Door nurtures relationships and supports recreational and happy activities. Should we use the previous chart, we will see that the deity residing in the Rest Door is the Surging Snake. In the near future, this may lessen the good effect of the Rest Door for this couple, since the Surging Snake represents lies and conflicts.

In a Lion Dance utilising Qi Men, there are other Qi Men aspects that can be taken into consideration besides the Doors. In this chart, we are also taking in the Six Harmony's occurrence into consideration. Six Harmony is frequently used in support of marriage because its occurrence and the activation of its energy will greatly help the couple in the long run.

In this specific chart (20 January 2016 at 3.00pm), the Six Harmony occurs in the Scenery Door which is an auspicious combination. The Scenery Door will promote the couple's attractiveness to each other and help their socialisation process, while Six Harmony is there to make sure both ends will meet. In the use of Lion Dance for marriage, the Doors that are not of use to the marriage can be left untouched.

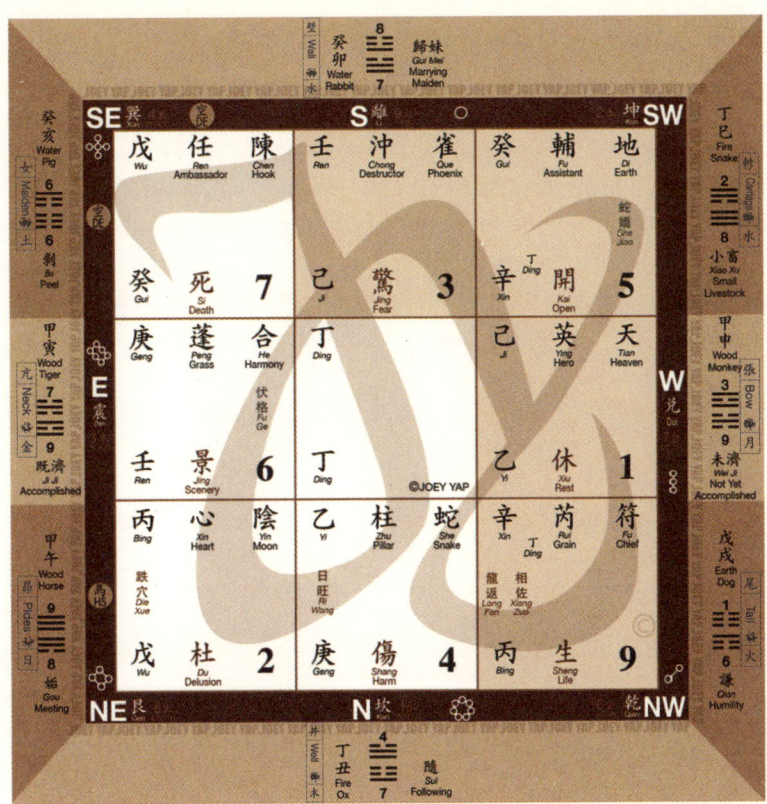

John's Chart 3

Here we suggest that John use the Life Door, Open Door, Rest Door and Scenery Door (Six Harmony). John can start the Lion Dance after he has planned the sequence. The male lion, which represents him as the breadwinner of the household, should be placed at the Open Door to symbolise the presence of more opportunities ahead for him.

The female lion which represents his wife, should be placed at the Life Door since channelling the Door's power will promote fertility for John to start a family with his wife.

Unique Lion Dance Formations

As previously mentioned, *Cai Qing* formations for the Lion Dance are only limited by imagination. There are therefore several other ways with which your story can be ritualised. Nonetheless, there are several formations that are not used very often and have been grouped under "special occasions only". Many of these came about in response to the need for having specific formations to go with specific festivals and circumstances.

Let's have a look at some of them in the next few pages.

Lion Dance Prosperity Formation
(*Shi Wu Cui Wang* 獅舞催旺)

As the name suggests, the prosperity formation helps you prosper. Whether you are a businessman or an employee, you will definitely need the Nobleman's help to move your endeavours ahead. Here is an example of a prosperity formation for channelling the cosmic favour of the Nobleman.

Formation	Six Harmony Nobleman Formation (*Liu He Gui Ren Qing Zhen* 六合貴人青陣)
Ingredients	12 mandarin oranges at least (up to 30 may be used depending on the customisation), 12 skewer sticks, 12 pieces of red paper (to be attached to the skewer sticks) with each one labelled with the 12 animal signs of the Chinese zodiac, 12 Nobleman papers (*Gui Ren Zhi* 貴人紙), 12 lettuces and a red envelope.

The Dance:

1. Put the 12 mandarin oranges on the floor as shown in the picture, with each orange embedded with a stick labelled with a red paper symbolic of one of the 12 Chinese zodiacs. The 12 pieces of red paper must be placed following the exact *Luo Pan*/Compass directions of their respective 12 animal signs. Place one Nobleman paper and one lettuce under each orange. In the middle of this circle, a round tray is to be filled with six oranges, silver coins, candies, a pomelo, a lettuce, and a red envelope.

2. The lion will first inspect the formation. Next, he will collect all the oranges, lettuces, and Nobleman papers in the order of the labels and head for the round tray in the middle.

3. The lion will keep these labelled oranges to itself and place all the collected lettuces and Nobleman papers under the big saucer. The lion will start giving away some of the oranges (not all), coins and candies on the saucer to the audience while playing with them. He will then slice open the pomelo into a flower shape and place it back in the saucer.

4. The candies, oranges and coins that previously surrounded the pomelo will now be replaced with the zodiac-marked mandarin oranges. The lion pairs them up as the following; Rat-Ox, Tiger-Pig, Rabbit-Dog, Dragon-Rooster, Snake-Monkey and Horse-Goat, and uses them to surround the opened pomelo. These pairings are based on the BaZi principles known as the Six Harmony (*Liu He* 六合).

5. The lion will peel the leftover oranges and use the skin to form different wordplay phrases at the petitioner's wish or instruction. It could be one of these phrases; Prospering Business (*Sheng Yi Shing Long* 生意興隆), Radiant Wealth (*Cai Yun Heng Tong* 財運亨通), Everything Goes Well (*Shi Shi Shun Li* 事事順利) or any other specially requested customisation. This phrase will be arranged on the floor in front of the saucer.

6. The lion will now bring the tray filled with the labelled oranges and opened pomelo back to the petitioner.

7. Special emphasis can be placed on the animal sign of the petitioner, or if the petitioner needs to attract a certain Nobleman, the emphasis can be placed on that Nobleman's animal sign.

8. When this formation is coupled with the correct Qi Men Hour and direction, the benefits can be expected to manifest quickly.

Meaning of the Formation:

The Nobleman carves the path, and hence the business will prosper (*Gui Ren Kai Lu, Sheng Yi Xing Long* 貴人開路，生意興隆).

Lion Triumphs Over Evil
(*Shi Wu Fu Mo* 獅舞伏魔)

The "Lion Triumphs Over Evil" is used to break bad formations. This is a ritual exclusive to the Lion Dance since the lion is considered an agent of Heaven and is able to save anyone. While the Snake and Crab formations are also able to remove negative Qi, those formations are entity-based.

The prevention of upcoming calamity and disaster is a different matter, since these are all negative Qi that lacks a point of focus. How then, can this be overcome? The influence of this negative Qi can be broken through the setup of the right formation. It also requires the use of the correct lion, since depending on how strong the negative Qi is, more than one warrior lion may be required. The lion should also be fierce and angry, such as the *Zhang Fei* Lion 張飛獅.

Formation	Breaking the Seven Killing Formation (破七煞陣)
Ingredients	7 roof tiles, 8 red packets, one round saucer to be filled with pineapple, lettuce, 12 mandarin oranges or more and candies.

Reminder: The Big-Head Buddha is needed in this formation.

The Dance:

1. The seven tiles are put on the floor with a red packet under each as shown in picture. These tiles are placed wherever a negative Qi Men sector is identified, which is usually where the Surging Snake or the Black Tortoise is found. A tray is placed not far away from the tiles, with the pineapple set upright in it and the lettuce and another red packet placed underneath it. The pineapple is then surrounded by mandarin oranges and candies.

2. The enraged lion first inspects the formation. The lion then starts breaking the tiles from the bottom to the top, and takes the red packets under the tiles as it moves along. Breaking the tiles represents breaking the negative Structures (*Po Zhen* 破陣). This way it slowly makes his way to the tray.

3. When he reaches the tray, it will throw the extra mandarin oranges (keeping 12 for later use) and candies to the crowd. The lion will then eat the pineapple and lettuce. He will shower the lettuce over the audience, while keeping one head of lettuce intact for later use. As for the pineapple, the lion returns it to the saucer surrounded by three red packets (the rest will be kept by the troupe).

4. Now the lion will split the 12 mandarin oranges into flowers and surround the pineapple and red packets with the oranges. The rest of the oranges will be skinned and this skin is used to form the wordplay "Great Fortune (*Da Ji* 大吉)" on the ground not far from the saucer. Firecrackers may also be lit to activate the Chief 直符, Life Door 生門 or Open Door 開門 of the Qi Men Chart.

5. The Big-Headed Buddha will pick up the tray and lead the lion into the petitioner's house to the praying altar. The tray will be placed on a surface in front of the altar, followed by the Big-Headed Buddha lighting one incense stick. At this point, the Big-Headed Buddha will take the lead and together with the lion, bow three times to the petitioner's Patron Deity.

6. To complete the ritual, the last head of lettuce will be returned to the petitioner to signify the regrowth of life.

Lion Dance Formations for Industries (*Shi Wu Wang Ye* 獅舞旺業)

Sometimes even if the business is decent, a little boost or additional prosperity would be nice. However, since it is not the beginning of the year, a New Year Formation is out of the picture and there really is not a bad formation that needs to be broken. For such an instance, there are the Lion Dance Formations for Industries.

Of course, there are so many industries that it would be impossible to list them all. Keep in mind that a grand and hugely plotted formation is not necessary to getting rich from your business. Your business will prosper, as long as you are blessed by the agents of Heaven.

Here are some options for business owners who wish to utilise Qi Men in Lion Dance to improve their businesses.

- Those working in the wine industry should call upon the power of the black *Zhang Fei* Lion 張飛獅. The *Zhang Fei* Lion represents bravery and leadership skills, and is usually portrayed as having an irascible and scrappy personality. This makes it ideal for the highly competitive wine industry which frequently entails severe competition, both in sales and sourcing high quality products. Calling upon the power of the Black Lion gives you tougher strength to stand your ground and fight your way through to success.

- If you own a law firm, call upon the power of the black-red, *Guan Yu* Lion 關羽獅. Whenever laws are concerned, this lion favours justice and is culturally well-known for his bravery and loyalty. Metaphysically speaking, seeking *Guan Yu*'s power to enhance your law firm's value within the time space continuum, will in reality allow you to attract more businesses by demonstrating that you know your values and what you are doing.

- If your industrial background is a think tank or consulting firm, call upon the power of the green, *Zhao Yun* Lion 趙雲獅. While *Guan Yu* and *Zhang Fei* are both fierce warrior-type lions, *Zhao Yun* is less temperamental and rational type of warrior in comparison, yet highly capable and successful. A consulting firm strives to provide the best solutions for their clients, therefore a Qi Men activation by the *Zhao Yun* Lion's character and glorious history is bound to be the best choice for this kind of firm.

- Those running a multi-generational family business also have a way of boosting their business. The yellow *Huang Zhong* Lion 黃忠獅 is ideal for this type of business due to his having served in the military for three generations in his past life, unmatched by anyone else. This lion symbolises stability and can help sustain the business for more generations. Of course, since the Lion Dance can be customised, one can use the *Huang Zhong* Lion to sustain the business and a different lion to bring industry-specific wealth.

- There are those who have single-handedly managed their institution, organisation or company for a long time and are currently at an advanced age that is nearing a milestone celebration. These hardworking and dedicated people can call upon the power of the wisest Lion, the *Liu Bei* Lion 劉備獅. The *Liu Bei* Lion is here to bless their journey, whether they are retiring, moving on or persisting with their efforts. This is the best time for them to take credit for their achievements and contributions, for this Lion Dance commands appreciation and respect from the masses. In the celebration of their efforts, good Qi is stirred up and can help the institution continue to thrive.

As this chapter comes to a close, we hope that the Art of Lion Dance and its application with Qi Men have been made clearer. The formations presented here, though already substantial, are only a small sample of the vast number of selections available in this deep and varied art.

The Hour Chart Structures showcase the real essence of where and when the dance should be performed. This is one of the most important aspects of the Lion Dance, since invoking the formation on a wrong date, at a wrong time and in a wrong direction will result in a wasted effort on your part.

Chapter 6

Hiring a Troupe for Qi Men Lion Dance

Having covered much of what there is to know about the Lion Dance, from the past to the present, from the mundane to the extraordinary, I hope that you have gained a solid fundamental knowledge of the Lion Dance. Here's to using this knowledge to plan a Lion Dance performance for an auspicious event or special day. Not only are you now well-versed in the cultural and historical aspects of the Lion Dance, I also seek to show you its metaphysical importance, and now would be the perfect time to put them both to use.

Though in the past the metaphysical aspect of the Lion Dance would also have been left to the troupe to plot and plan, today, martial arts troupes focus more on the martial arts aspect of the performance than going into the metaphysical. So while they are able to dance the formations and perform the steps, some details, such as determining the time and place based on a Qi Men Chart is down to you.

They will still be able to perform to good effect without these details, but by doing some of the legwork, you can be assured that the performance is tailored to your needs and situation alone. While you may be able to consult a Qi Men or Feng Shui practitioner for confirmation, keep in mind that even they may not be familiar with the relationship between the Lion Dance and Qi Men Dun Jia!

Therefore, as someone who now comprehends the best of both arts, it is now part of your responsibility to make sure that when the troupe arrives, you can properly guide them to maximise the results of summoning your auspicious luck. In this concluding chapter, I have prepared a list of frequently asked questions to expound on some trivia and information in an effort to clear up any misinformation that may arise regarding the art of Qi Men Lion Dance.

Lion Dance and Dragon Dance performers.

What's the difference between a Lion Dance and a Dragon Dance?

Those familiar with both the Lion Dance and other Chinese festival traditions may wonder why the lion is favoured over the dragon (in some cases). After all, the Dragon Dance is just as well-known, and the dragon as the symbol of the emperor gives the impression of even greater power and influence, so shouldn't one use a dragon instead of a lion?

Well, for one, these two mythical creatures are beyond comparison. Both dances are considered auspicious and meant to bring luck and dispel evil. They are used in the consecration of temples, the officialising of new buildings and other constructions, the inauguration of activities, events and businesses, the sowing and harvesting of crops, religious and ceremonial festivals, secular celebrations and a variety of other events and milestones, the possibilities are endless.

Of course, there are clear differences between these two dances. The most obvious would be the size, and the power and presence of the performing animal. In a Lion Dance ritual or performance, the animal itself is controlled by two persons, one at the head and one at the back. Though they may also be joined by a Big-Headed Buddha, as well as a percussion team, the lion itself requires only a team of two. Meanwhile, due to the dragon's size and length, a team of 15 persons is usually required. There are even behemoth dragons that would require a crew of up to a hundred to control and manoeuvre!

Since the Lion Dance requires only a small space, the space can be personalised according to the formation planned and therefore, ritualised in a story. Thus, the space and ritual can be modified to suit very specific goals and objectives according to one's own personal interests and needs. Of course, should one have the space for it, one could certainly go for a Dragon Dance. The Dragon Dance may in fact be ideal for large spaces such as halls and factories, or should the negative Qi to be dispersed is overly powerful. When it comes down to it, the main factors are space and need, and once they have been determined, a professional team can advise on the more pertinent issues of formations and rituals.

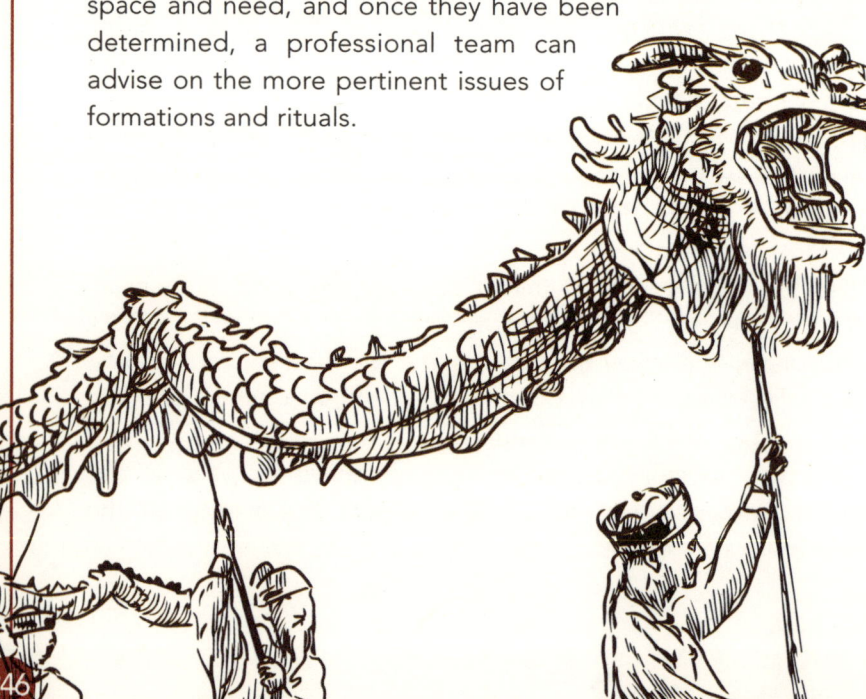

Lion Dance competitors in action.

Is it possible to incorporate Qi Men aspects into a competitive Lion Dance 跳椿 routine?

Competitive Lion Dance focuses on technical skills, agility and stunts. Therefore, the steps, movements and stunts they perform are more suited to that purpose than for a Qi Men ritual. Keep in mind that Competitive Lion Dance requires a lot of space and a huge set up that will need some work and will likely cost a lot. The focus on stunt work, and reduced emphasis on rituals, such as *Cai Qing* 採青 will make it harder for the troupe to adjust their routine to break a Bad Qi formation, or to activate a good one.

Unlike the functional or ritualistic Lion Dance where the focus is to "Pluck the Greens", the Competitive Lion Dance is judged in three main categories: *Gao* 高, how high and how far is the dance team able to jump forward in each leap and with what degree of grace and ease; *Xian* 險, how risky and dangerous the manoeuvres are; and *Nan* 難, the degree of difficulty of the movements or stunts. Therefore, the purposes of Competitive Lion Dance are generally restricted by martial arts academies to entertainment and trophy-winning or prestige only.

Aside from that, it can be tricky to hire a troupe to perform competitive Lion Dance for functional and Qi Men purposes. Though martial arts academies clearly delineated competitive teams from performative teams, there are a few academies with troupes capable of both. Keep in mind that due to the incredible talents of the competitive performers, their fee is likely to be higher than that of a normal performance only Lion Dance troupe.

Unless the Lion Dance troupe is well-trained and famous for their stunts, it is best to avoid overly complicated and dangerous stunts, especially for *Gao Qing*. Not only does a dangerous setup endanger the dancers, from a Qi Men perspective, should the lion fall and the dancers are injured during the performance, it could be a bad omen for you. However, their success in performing these overly dangerous stunts would depict your ability to overcome difficult obstacles, which is a phenomenal symbolic representation – provided that you have first set up the correct formation and picked the right timing.

How long do performers have to train before they can perform Lion Dance?

When you hire someone to carry out a strategic execution that will make a noticeable impact on your life, you do want to be assured that they know what they are doing, and that they will not mess up and bring you bad fortune instead. Therefore, you should hire a troupe with experience, one that is already fairly established and has a good reputation.

In olden days, the Lion Dance was taught by martial arts academies, and it remains the same today. However, nowadays the Lion Dance is likely to be taught as an optional course, therefore, not all martial artists are able to perform the dance. In the past, lion dancing was only open to men, but today, women are allowed to participate too, though mixed lions (controlled by a man and a woman) are rare. While today it is possible for people to learn the Lion Dance for recreational purposes, back then it was a way of making a living, and so martial arts academies would only select the fittest and healthiest men with the proper attitude.

Some of the selective criteria are:

1. Possess good attitude, behaviour and temperament
2. Healthy and fit
3. Respectful, rule-abiding, willing to accept instructions and criticisms
4. Willing to preserve traditions and customs
5. Reliable and trustworthy

Young Lion Dance performers rehearsing before a performance.

Training begins with the basics, from various stationary stances to steps and more elaborate movements. Training is first based on drills and repetitions until the student has perfected the stance and moves and knows them by heart. Although monotonous, this activity builds strength and patience, and lets the Master (*Shi Fu* 師傅) weed out those who lack the perseverance, determination and self-discipline. By doing so, one can find the quickest, most graceful and most agile of his students, who would be promoted to roles in the Lion Dance.

Once the student has been deemed skillful enough to participate in Lion Dance, both experienced and less experienced performers will perform together. The more experienced members are the ones in charge of the main lion which performs *Cai Qing* and other stunts and rituals. Newer Lion Dance performers will take charge of the secondary lion or secondary instruments such as the cymbals and the gong. Their roles will rotate from performance to performance as they hone their skills and gain experience until they become skilled enough to handle the main lion head or the drums.

With so much effort going into a performance, how much am I required to pay the Lion Dance troupe?

It differs from troupe to troupe and prices can fluctuate wildly. If the troupe is associated with a reputable cultural organisation, it is likely to charge more than the "rogue" troupes, which are not registered and command lower prices for inferior quality dances. That said, even under an organisation, Lion Dance troupes are frequently underpaid. More than often, their fare is just enough to cover transport costs and maintenance for their equipment. Many troupe members learn the art and perform out of love for the art and the culture surrounding it, since it is very hard to make a living out of lion dancing nowadays.

Therefore, it is good to keep in mind that you are paying for the best, since troupes train for years just to get up to performance level. If they are performing, they are already deemed highly skilled. It also depends on the kind of performance you have requested. *Gao Qing* will likely cost more since it poses greater risk and more preparation for the performers. Therefore, should your financial situation permit, you can be generous with the payment.

The troupe is usually paid with a cheque inside a red envelope used during *Cai Qing*. Sometimes the troupe can also use an invoice. In addition, you are expected to give a red packet to every performer, so make sure to confirm how many of them will be showing up for the performance. If you are organising a Lion Dance for a house-warming party or for an event where food is served, you may wonder if you will need to order extra food for the troupe. Note that the Lion Dance troupe will usually not stay for food, since it is considered common courtesy for them to complete their performance and leave. However, if you invite them to eat, they will likely be glad to accept your offer.

Can I request the use of a Northern Lion for my Lion Dance with Qi Men aspects?

At first glance the difference between the Northern Lion and the Southern Lion may seem merely aesthetic. The Southern Lion is more intricately decorated while the Northern Lion resembles a Pekingese dog, also known in the West as a *Fu* Dog. The Northern Lions have longer coat and more defined and expressive faces.

Even their movements and steps differ from those of the Southern Lion. Southern Lion Dance movements are closely related to martial arts, and therefore include a lot of leaps and stunts. Northern Lions however are more playful and their performances generally involve acts such as tumbling, chasing things and balancing on a ball.

That does not mean that Northern Lions are not suitable for the solemn Qi Men purposes. However, keep in mind that Southern Lion Dance performers are far more commonly found in most places, so due to supply and demand, hiring a Northern Lion Dance troupe may incur higher expenses. Also make sure to check with the troupe if they are able and willing to perform the more ritualistic movements and steps of a Lion Dance with Qi Men. Otherwise, there is no reason why you should not hire a Northern Lion Dance troupe.

I understood that there are Qi Men components other than the Doors and Stem-Stem combinations. Can you explain what they are?

The 8 Deities, also known as the 8 Gods, govern the Spirit Realm. There are 10 Deities in total but only eight of them appear in a single Qi Men chart. Each deity has his or her own attributes for helping your strategies in a unique way. They represent the spiritual energies and forces within the universe that impact the affairs of man. The energy of the Spirit Realm is in constant communication with the natural world around us and the strength of the energy can be observed by looking at the Seven Stars Path in the Qi Men chart.

Through the practice of Qi Men, we are able to gain insight into these interactions and understand how the Spirit Realm influences the outcomes of our Lion Dance. Equally, we may also comprehend how to direct the energies of the Spirit Realm to help us achieve our goals.

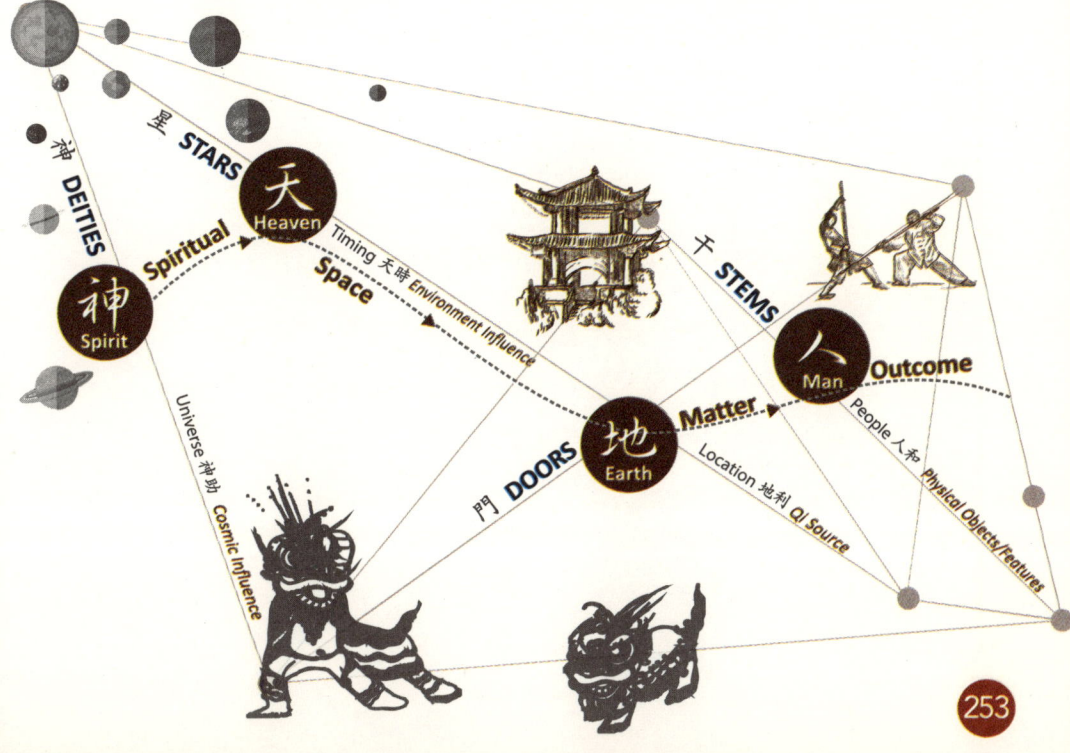

Deities	Auspicious for
Chief 直符	• Seeking fame and fortune • Seeking better employment opportunities • Seeking help and support from Noble people or mentors • Increasing one's wealth • Construction and renovation • Building up an establishment
Surging Snake 騰蛇	Inauspicious. Avoid it under usual circumstances. Useful for: • Causing trouble, rocking the boat, stirring up unpleasant things • Deceiving, cheating, or confusing the enemy • Occult or spiritual activities • Promoting an idea or influencing one's enemies
Great Moon 太陰	• Seeking knowledge and wisdom • Academic activities • Taking up a new job position • Strategising and planning • Hiding or seeking refuge, avoiding ambushes
Six Harmony 六合	• Marriages • Happy occasions • Peacemaking or brokering a peace treaty with others • Negotiations, dealings • Persuasions • Productions, transactions, intermediary activities, match-making matters
Grappling Hook 勾陳	Inauspicious. Avoid it under usual circumstances. Useful for: • Mental warfare • Litigation • Buying or selling properties • Setting up traps

Deities	Auspicious for
White Tiger 白虎	Inauspicious. Avoid it under usual circumstances. Useful for: • Seeking to win in sports • Increasing energy and stamina • Increasing fearlessness • Battle and warfare • Initiating a lawsuit against others
Red Phoenix 朱雀	Inauspicious. Avoid it under usual circumstances. Useful for: • Documentation, art • Winning arguments and disputes
Black Tortoise 玄武	Inauspicious. Avoid it under usual circumstances. Useful for: • Breaking bad habits • Undoing negative spirit influences • Unimportant endeavours, planning, conspiracies
Nine Earth 九地	• Staying undercover or hidden • Maintaining a low profile to avoid unwanted attention • Seeking to increase asset values and net worth • Passive income
Nine Heaven 九天	• Seeking fame and fortune • Seeking promotions • Executing plans • Launching strategies against one's opponents • Publicising issues • Achieving high status and rank • Meeting with a Nobleman • Establishing business contacts and making business deals

Other than the 8 Deities, we also have the 9 Stars which also affect the outcomes of your strategy.

We often say that a key component of success is the capacity to be in the right place, at the right time. The 9 Stars reflect the movements of celestial bodies which affect good fortune, and their relationships with the earth and humanity in turn, impact the effects of the factors of place and man.

Commonly, we observe these Stars for:

Stars	Auspicious for
Heavenly Grass 天蓬星	• Entrepreneurship • Innovations and reactions • Gaining knowledge and wisdom • Ideas – thinking, thoughts, planning, business plans • Cultivation and proper structuring • Organising things
Heavenly Grain 天芮星	• Mentorship • Service of something or someone • Encouraging socialising and building relationships • Team building • Training, teaching and recruiting • Pursuing wealth
Heavenly Destructor 天冲星	• All forms of athletic pursuits • Making the first strike • Direct confrontations • Speculative luck • Carrying out charitable works or donations • Making the first move to build friendships and expand social circles
Heavenly Assistant 天辅星	• Education • Academic pursuits • Scholarly creations and projects • Studying and learning skills • Reading

Stars	Auspicious for
Heavenly Bird 天禽星	• Leadership • Gathering support in pursuit of common goals • Creating social cohesion • Praying to deities for wishes • Initiating new plans that need immediate support
Heavenly Heart 天心星	• Seeking medical cures or treatments for ailments • Healing • Rejuvenation • Marriage • Carrying out plans or strategies
Heavenly Pillar 天柱星	• Crafting speeches • Making public speeches • Encouragements • Raising morale • Strengthening strategies
Heavenly Ambassador 天任星	• Managing people • Sorting out money-related issues, such as obtaining licences, paying off and collecting debts, giving to charity, making purchases and investments
Heavenly Hero 天英星	• Taking the lead on the front line • Achieving grand schemes and great ideas • Improving brand names or images • Instilling good names or reputations • Volunteering • Being seen or getting noticed

When selecting the right Hour Chart for your Qi Men Lion Dance performance, by looking at the Stars and Deities along with the Doors, will provide you with more detailed view of the possible actions that can be taken, along with the outcomes that can be expected. For example, having the Nine Heaven in a favourable sector (one with a good Door) creates the opportunity for that sector to be activated with *Gao Qing*, a physical ascension that will hopefully lead to the metaphorical ascension of good fortune. Likewise, taking these components into consideration gives you a greater understanding of the various structures that may appear in the Hour Chart, and thus, also gives you a better idea of which sectors to favour and which to avoid in the Lion Dance.

How do I know if I need a special formation?

A variety of Qi Men Lion Dance formations are included in this book. If you find that at first glance none of them meet your needs, keep in mind that most of these formations are highly customisable. Depending on the situation you are facing or what you need the Lion Dance for, the formations can be further customised and specialised.

If you are not sure where to begin, start planning your Lion Dance performance by selecting your best Personal Date and Hour using the Qi Men Hour Chart system. Inform the troupe of your selection and decision so they can plan their performance accordingly. If their leader is familiar with metaphysics, he may also assist you further, by selecting the right formations and movements. Some troupes may even have the skill to do a personal selection for you, but they may not know what to do with a Qi Men Hour Chart.

To begin with, there are 1080 Qi Men charts in total, each of them yields different outcomes, therefore, requiring different strategies and approaches. This gives you a huge variety of options in the first place. In this book I have provided 24 of the most common Qi Men Formations for you to refer to. The 24 formations in this book have been rated from excellent to malicious to make you aware of exactly what they can do for you. This way, you can clearly identify the favourable and unfavourable charts for proper planning of your Lion Dance Strategic Execution.

Anything that is empowered by the lion is considered auspicious, so even if the Qi Men Hour Chart you have selected suggests a formation breaking, this action will still likely work in your favour. The Qi Men Hour Chart simply suggests the best strategy for you to follow. Even by allowing the action to happen, the lion will channel the auspicious Qi to manipulate luck in your favour.

However, if you find that none of the charts seem right for your situation, or if you are uncertain about modifying any of the formations found in this book, it would be best to consult with a metaphysics practitioner specialising in Qi Men Dun Jia before you start. Another option would be to refer to our Qi Men Dun Jia Compendium and Qi Men Dun Jia Strategic Execution reference books which offer more detailed explanations on each chart and the various components found within.

If martial arts schools have their own symbol or flag, how do I distinguish their identity?

The best way to identify them is by looking at the flag flying at the performance. There are three types of flags in general. All three of them are inherited from the Chinese battlefield. Traditionally, all three of them come together every time a troupe is out to perform. Today, however, this may not be the case.

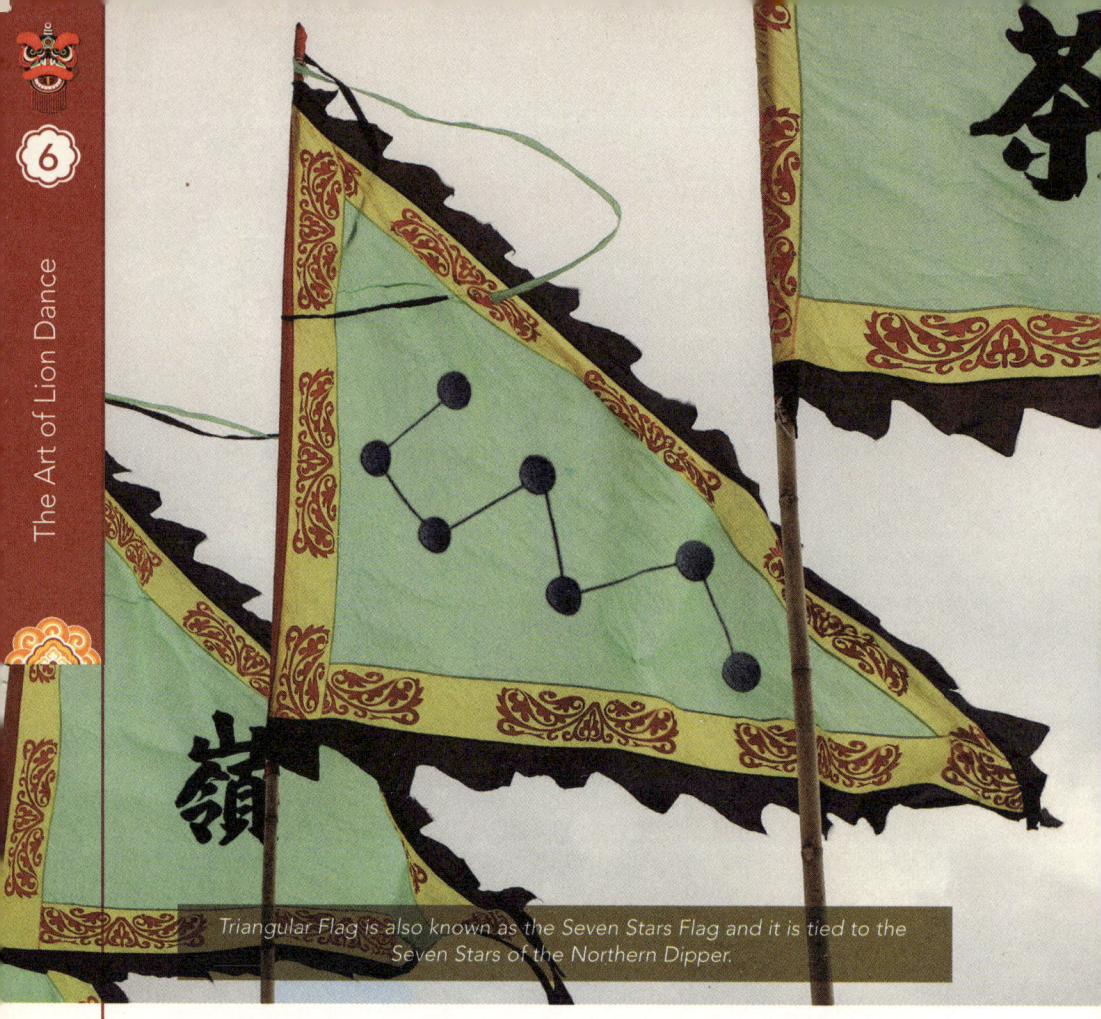

Triangular Flag is also known as the Seven Stars Flag and it is tied to the Seven Stars of the Northern Dipper.

Triangular Flag (*San Jiao Qi* 三角旗)

The triangular flag is also known as the Seven Stars Flag. This is an ordinary Chinese flag in the battlefield. This flag came to be known as the Seven Stars Flag for the seven dots that can be found on it. It is also tied to the Seven Stars of the Northern Dipper. The Seven Stars Flags of today are usually embroidered with the martial art school's logo instead of the seven dots.

War Flag or Rally Flag is printed with the name of a particular troupe.

The War Flag or Rally Flag
(*Ri Zi Qi* 日字旗 / *Biao Qi* 髟旗 / *Zhan Qi* 戰旗)

This is a short flag on a long stick. This flag used to be flown by the troops as they charged at the enemy on the battlefield, especially since the design permitted it to be carried on horseback. Nowadays, this flag is printed with the name of the troupe.

In the olden days, the General's Flag was a major distinguishing work of a troupe.

The General's Flag (*Shuai Qi* 帥旗)

The General's Flag is meant to stoke a martial arts school's morale as it used to on the battlefields of old. This is one big flag accompanied by two couplets at the sides. Back in the olden days, the General's Flag was the major distinguishing mark of a troupe. In the modern era, the flag is no longer so intricately tied to the troupe's identity. Back then, in order to accurately identify the particular martial arts school or clan of the Lion Dance troupe, one had to read and decipher the couplets hanging with the flag.

An example would be this couplet: "英棍飛騰龍擺尾，雄拳放出虎昂頭", which translates to, "Graceful staff moving like the dragon swings the tail, strong fist releases outwards as the tiger raises its head." It means that this troupe practices *Chai Li Fuo*'s 蔡李佛 fist-focused martial arts.

Epilogue

The Lion Dance is a particularly favourite subject of mine which goes way back to my childhood years. Even in the present day, it has become a habit and traditional practice for me to have a Lion Dance performance done annually at my offices and home in order to usher in the positive energies of a brand new Lunar Year. In the course of writing this book, my research has also revealed much more than I imagined about the Lion Dance itself as a whole. I hope all this knowledge of which I have presented in this book is as engaging it was for you as it was for me.

No doubt, its ties with Qi Men Dun Jia – another favourite subject of mine – is something which is not known by many. While the lay audience is aware of the Lion Dance's primary purpose in inaugurating many official events, nobody (except maybe some traditional performers) knows the metaphysical science behind of how it works. Qi Men Dun Jia is not only a remarkable tool for reading the natural energies present in our lives, it is also powerful instrument in providing us with means to implement strategies in order to achieve the best possible results. It seems only natural that through its evolution in traditional Daoist practices that it became interwoven with the Lion Dance – a cultural dance which is also deeply rooted in ancient shamanic practices.

If you are new to the practice of Qi Men Dun Jia or have a fascination with Chinese culture, I hope this book has lit a spark in you on the former and enriched your knowledge on the latter. It has always been my passion and my life's goal to share with the world the incredible possibilities of what Chinese Metaphysics have to offer. In the line of my work, my travels to China often take me to a lot of places which reveal many interesting stories about traditional culture and practices which are still often practised by the Chinese diaspora today.

It is in this frame of mind that gave me the inspiration to come up with a Chinese cultural series to preserve the rich Chinese heritage and present them to an international audience. The Art of Lion Dance is the first of what I hope to be many more books in the same vein that will not only bring to light many fascinating information and stories, but also reveal how these cultural practices are intertwined deeply with Chinese Metaphysics. While it is by no means the most comprehensive book on subject, I have presented it in what I hope is the best possible way to introduce it to a whole new generation. Hopefully it will give you a deeper appreciation for the Lion Dance. Therefore, the next time you have the opportunity to catch a performance, you will be able to view it in a whole new light.

JOEY YAP'S QI MEN DUN JIA Reference Series

Qi Men Dun Jia Compendium Second edition

Qi Men Dun Jia 540 Yang Structure

Qi Men Dun Jia 540 Yin Structure

Qi Men Dun Jia Year Charts

Qi Men Dun Jia Month Charts

Qi Men Dun Jia Day Charts

Qi Men Dun Jia Day Charts (San Yuan Method)

Qi Men Dun Jia Forecasting Method (Book 1)

Qi Men Dun Jia Forecasting Method (Book 2)

Qi Men Dun Jia Evidential Occurrences

Qi Men Dun Jia Destiny Analysis

Qi Men Dun Jia Feng Shui

Qi Men Dun Jia Date, Time & Activity Selection

Qi Men Dun Jia Annual Destiny Analysis

Qi Men Dun Jia Strategic Executions

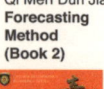
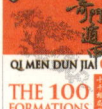
Qi Men Dun Jia The 100 Formations

Qi Men Dun Jia Sun Tzu Warcraft

Qi Men Dun Jia 28 Constellations

Qi Men Dun Jia The Deities

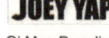
Qi Men Dun Jia The Stars

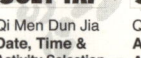
Qi Men Dun Jia The Doors

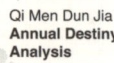

Qi Men Dun Jia The Stems

This is the most comprehensive reference series to Qi Men Dun Jia in the Chinese Metaphysics world. Exhaustively written for the purpose of facilitating studies and further research, this collection of reference texts and educational books aims to bridge the gap for students who want to learn, and the teachers who want to teach Qi Men.

These essential references provide practical guidance for all branches under the Qi Men Dun Jia studies including Destiny Analysis, Feng Shui, Strategic Executions and Forecasting method.

These books are available exclusively at:
store.joeyyap.com

JOEY YAP'S
QI MEN DUN JIA MASTERY PROGRAM

This is the world's most comprehensive training program on the subject of Qi Men Dun Jia. Joey Yap is the Qi Men Strategist for some of Asia's wealthiest tycoons. This program is modelled after Joey Yap's personal application methods, covering techniques and strategies he applies for his high net worth clients. There is a huge difference between studying the subject as a scholar and learning how to use it successfully as a Qi Men strategist. In this program, Joey Yap shares with you what he personally uses to transform his own life and the lives of million others. In other words, he shares with his students what actually works and not just what looks good in theory with no real practical value. This means that the program covers his personal trade secrets in using the art of Qi Men Dun Jia.

There are five unique programs, with each of them covering one specific application aspect of the Joey Yap's Qi Men Dun Jia system.

Joey Yap's training program focuses on getting results. Theories and formulas are provided in the course workbook so that valuable class time are not wasted dwelling on formulas. Each course comes with its own comprehensive 400-plus pages workbook. Taught once a year exclusively by Joey Yap, seats to these programs are extremely limited.

Call +6(03) 2284 8080 or
email courses@masteryacademy.com for enquiries

JOEY YAP CONSULTING GROUP

Pioneering Metaphysics-Centric Personal and Corporate Consultations

Founded in 2002, the Joey Yap Consulting Group is the pioneer in the provision of metaphysics-driven coaching and consultation services for professionals and individuals alike. Under the leadership of the renowned international Chinese Metaphysics consultant, author and trainer, Dato' Joey Yap, it has become a world-class specialised metaphysics consulting firm with a strong presence in four continents, meeting the metaphysics-centric needs of its A-list clientele, ranging from celebrities to multinational corporations.

The Group's core consultation practice areas include Feng Shui, BaZi and Qi Men Dun Jia, which are complemented by ancillary services such as Date Selection, Face Reading and Yi Jing. Its team of highly trained professional consultants, led by its Chief Consultant, Dato' Joey Yap, is well-equipped with unparalleled knowledge and experience to help clients achieve their ultimate potentials in various fields and specialisations. Given its credentials, the Group is certainly the firm of choice across the globe for metaphysics-related consultations.

The Peerless Industry Expert

Benchmarked against the standards of top international consulting firms, our consultants work closely with our clients to achieve the best possible outcomes. The possibilities are infinite as our expertise extends from consultations related to the forces of nature under the subject of Feng Shui, to those related to Destiny Analysis and effective strategising under BaZi and Qi Men Dun Jia respectively.

To date, we have consulted a great diversity of clients, ranging from corporate clients – from various industries such as real estate, finance and telecommunication, amongst others – to the hundreds of thousands of individuals in their key life aspects. Adopting up-to-date and pragmatic approaches, we provide comprehensive services while upholding the importance of clients' priorities and effective outcomes. Recognised as the epitome of Chinese Metaphysics, we possess significant testimonies from worldwide clients as a trusted Brand.

www.joeyyap.com | +6(03) - 2284 8080

Feng Shui Consultation

Residential Properties
- Initial Land/Property Assessment
- Residential Feng Shui Consultation
- Residential Land Selection
- End-to-End Residential Consultation

Commercial Properties
- Initial Land/Property Assessment
- Commercial Feng Shui Consultation
- Commercial Land Selection
- End-to-End Commercial Consultation

Property Developers
- End-to-End Consultation
- Post-Consultation Advisory Services
- Panel Feng Shui Consultant

Property Investors
- Your Personal Feng Shui Consultant
- Tailor-Made Packages

Memorial Parks & Burial Sites
- Yin House Feng Shui

BaZi Consultation

Personal Destiny Analysis
- Individual BaZi Analysis
- BaZi Analysis for Families

Strategic Analysis for Corporate Organizations
- BaZi Consultations for Corporations
- BaZi Analysis for Human Resource Management

Entrepreneurs and Business Owners
- BaZi Analysis for Entrepreneurs

Career Pursuits
- BaZi Career Analysis

Relationships
- Marriage and Compatibility Analysis
- Partnership Analysis

General Public
- Annual BaZi Forecast
- Your Personal BaZi Coach

Date Selection Consultation

- Marriage Date Selection
- Caesarean Birth Date Selection
- House-Moving Date Selection
- Renovation and Groundbreaking Dates
- Signing of Contracts
- Official Openings
- Product Launches

Qi Men Dun Jia Consultation

Strategic Execution
- Business and Investment Prospects

Forecasting
- Wealth and Life Pursuits
- People and Environmental Matters

Feng Shui
- Residential Properties
- Commercial Properties

Speaking Engagement

Many reputable organisations and institutions have worked closely with Joey Yap Consulting Group to build a synergistic business relationship by engaging our team of consultants, which are led by Joey Yap, as speakers at their corporate events.

We tailor our seminars and talks to suit the anticipated or pertinent group of audience. Be it department subsidiary, your clients or even the entire corporation, we aim to fit your requirements in delivering the intended message(s) across.

CHINESE METAPHYSICS REFERENCE SERIES

The Chinese Metaphysics Reference Series is a collection of reference texts, source material, and educational textbooks to be used as supplementary guides by scholars, students, researchers, teachers and practitioners of Chinese Metaphysics.

These comprehensive and structured books provide fast, easy reference to aid in the study and practice of various Chinese Metaphysics subjects including Feng Shui, BaZi, Yi Jing, Zi Wei, Liu Ren, Ze Ri, Ta Yi, Qi Men Dun Jia and Mian Xiang.

The Chinese Metaphysics Compendium

At over 1,000 pages, the Chinese Metaphysics Compendium is a unique one-volume reference book that compiles ALL the formulas relating to Feng Shui, BaZi (Four Pillars of Destiny), Zi Wei (Purple Star Astrology), Yi Jing (I-Ching), Qi Men (Mystical Doorways), Ze Ri (Date Selection), Mian Xiang (Face Reading) and other sources of Chinese Metaphysics.

It is presented in the form of easy-to-read tables, diagrams and reference charts, all of which are compiled into one handy book. This first-of-its-kind compendium is presented in both English and its original Chinese language, so that none of the meanings and contexts of the technical terminologies are lost.

The only essential and comprehensive reference on Chinese Metaphysics, and an absolute must-have for all students, scholars, and practitioners of Chinese Metaphysics.

			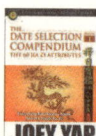	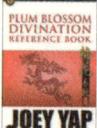			
The Ten Thousand Year Calendar (Pocket Edition)	The Ten Thousand Year Calendar	Dong Gong Date Selection	The Date Selection Compendium	Plum Blossoms Divination Reference Book	Xuan Kong Da Gua Ten Thousand Year Calendar	San Yuan Dragon Gate Eight Formations Water Method	

BaZi Hour Pillar Useful Gods - Wood	BaZi Hour Pillar Useful Gods - Fire	BaZi Hour Pillar Useful Gods - Earth	BaZi Hour Pillar Useful Gods - Metal	BaZi Hour Pillar Useful Gods - Water	Xuan Kong Da Gua Structures Reference Book	Xuan Kong Da Gua 64 Gua Transformation Analysis	
					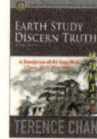		
BaZi Structures and Structural Useful Gods - Wood	BaZi Structures and Structural Useful Gods - Fire	BaZi Structures and Structural Useful Gods - Earth	BaZi Structures and Structural Useful Gods - Metal	BaZi Structures and Structural Useful Gods - Water	Earth Study Discern Truth Second Edition	Eight Mansions Bright Mirror	

Secret of Xuan Kong	Ode to Flying Stars	Xuan Kong Purple White Script	Ode to Mysticism	The Yin House Handbook	Water Water Everywhere	Xuan Kong Da Gua Not Exactly For Dummies	

www.masteryacademy.com | +6(03) - 2284 8080

SAN YUAN QI MEN XUAN KONG DA GUA Reference Series

San Yuan Qi Men Xuan Kong Da Gua **Compendium**

San Yuan Qi Men Xuan Kong Da Gua **540 Yang Structure**

San Yuan Qi Men Xuan Kong Da Gua **540 Yin Structure**

Xuan Kong Flying Star **Secrets Of The 81 Combinations**

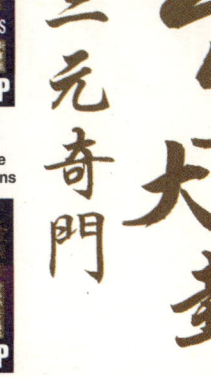

Xuan Kong Da Gua **Fixed Yao Method**

Xuan Kong Da Gua **Flying Yao Method**

Xuan Kong Da Gua **6 Relationships Method**

Xuan Kong Flying Star **Purple White Script's Advanced Star Charts**

The **San Yuan Qi Men Xuan Kong Da Gua Series** is written for the advanced learners in mind. Unlock the secrets to this highly exclusive art and seamlessly integrate both Qi Men Dun Jia and the Xuan Kong Da Gua 64 Hexagrams into one unified practice for effective applications.

This collection is an excellent companion for genuine enthusiasts, students and professional practitioners of the San Yuan Qi Men Xuan Kong Da Gua studies.

Xuan Kong Collection

Xuan Kong Flying Stars

This book is an essential introductory book to the subject of Xuan Kong Fei Xing, a well-known and popular system of Feng Shui. Learn 'tricks of the trade' and 'trade secrets' to enhance and maximise Qi in your home or office.

Xuan Kong Nine Life Star Series ((Available in English & Chinese versions)

Joey Yap's Feng Shui Essentials - The Xuan Kong Nine Life Star Series of books comprises of nine individual titles that provide detailed information about each individual Life Star.

Based on the complex and highly-evolved Xuan Kong Feng Shui system, each book focuses on a particular Life Star and provides you with a detailed Feng Shui guide.

Joey Yap's BaZi Profiling System

Three Levels of BaZi Profiling (English & Chinese versions)

In BaZi Profiling, there are three levels that reflect three different stages of a person's personal nature and character structure.

Level 1 – The Day Master

The Day Master in a nutshell is the basic you. The inborn personality. It is your essential character. It answers the basic question "who am I". There are ten basic personality profiles – the ten Day Masters – each with its unique set of personality traits, likes and dislikes.

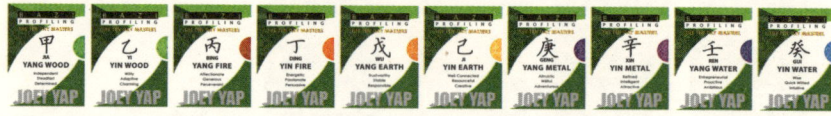

Level 2 – The Structure

The Structure is your behavior and attitude – in other words, it is about how you use your personality. It expands on the Day Master (Level 1). The structure reveals your natural tendencies in life – are you a controller, creator, supporter, thinker or connector? Each of the Ten Day Masters express themselves differently through the five Structures. Why do we do the things we do? Why do we like the things we like? The answers are in our BaZi Structure.

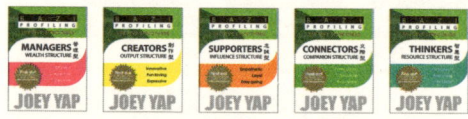

Level 3 – The Profile

The Profile depicts your role in your life. There are ten roles (Ten BaZi Profiles) related to us. As to each to his or her own - the roles we play are different from one another and it is unique to each Profile.

What success means to you, for instance, differs from your friends – this is similar to your sense of achievement or whatever you think of your purpose in life is.

Through the BaZi Profile, you will learn the deeper level of your personality. It helps you become aware of your personal strengths and works as a trigger for you to make all the positive changes to be a better version of you.

Keep in mind, only through awareness that you will be able to maximise your natural talents, abilities and skills. Only then, ultimately, you will get to enter into what we refer as 'flow' of life – a state where you have the powerful force to naturally succeed in life.

www.BaZiprofiling.com

THE BaZi 60 PILLARS SERIES

The BaZi 60 Pillars Series is a collection of ten volumes focusing on each of the Pillars or Jia Zi in BaZi Astrology. Learn how to see BaZi Chart in a new light through the Pictorial Method of BaZi analysis and elevate your proficiency in BaZi studies through this new understanding. Joey Yap's 60 Pillars Life Analysis Method is a refined and enhanced technique that is based on the fundamentals set by the true masters of olden times, and modified to fit to the sophistication of current times.

BaZi Collection

With these books, leading Chinese Astrology Master Trainer Joey Yap makes it easy to learn how to unlock your Destiny through your BaZi. BaZi or Four Pillars of Destiny is an ancient Chinese science which enables individuals to understand their personality, hidden talents and abilities, as well as their luck cycle - by examining the information contained within their birth data.

Understand and learn more about this accurate ancient science with this BaZi Collection.

BOOK 1   BOOK 2   BOOK 3   BOOK 4   BOOK 5   The 10 Gods

(Available in English & Chinese)

Feng Shui Collection

Design Your Legacy

Design Your Legacy is Joey Yap's first book on the profound subject of Yin House Feng Shui, which is the study Feng Shui for burials and tombs. Although it is still pretty much a hidden practice that is largely unexplored by modern literature, the significance of Yin House Feng Shui has permeated through the centuries – from the creation of the imperial lineage of emperors in ancient times to the iconic leaders who founded modern China.

This book unveils the true essence of Yin House Feng Shui with its significant applications that are unlike the myths and superstition which have for years, overshadowed the genuine practice itself. Discover how Yin House Feng Shui – the true precursor to all modern Feng Shui practice, can be used to safeguard the future of your descendants and create a lasting legacy.

Must-Haves for Property Analysis!

For homeowners, those looking to build their own home or even investors who are looking to apply Feng Shui to their homes, these series of books provides valuable information from the classical Feng Shui therioes and applications.

(Available in English & Chinese) (Available in English & Chinese)

In his trademark straight-to-the-point manner, Joey shares with you the Feng Shui do's and dont's when it comes to finding a property with favorable Feng Shui, which is condusive for home living.

Stories and Lessons on Feng Shui Series

All in all, this series is a delightful chronicle of Joey's articles, thoughts and vast experience - as a professional Feng Shui consultant and instructor - that have been purposely refined, edited and expanded upon to make for a light-hearted, interesting yet educational read. And with Feng Shui, BaZi, Mian Xiang and Yi Jing all thrown into this one dish, there's something for everyone.

(Available in English & Chinese)

More Titles under Joey Yap Books

Pure Feng Shui

Pure Feng Shui is Joey Yap's debut with an international publisher, CICO Books. It is a refreshing and elegant look at the intricacies of Classical Feng Shui - now compiled in a useful manner for modern day readers. This book is a comprehensive introduction to all the important precepts and techniques of Feng Shui practices.

Your Aquarium Here

This book is the first in Fengshuilogy Series, which is a series of matter-of-fact and useful Feng Shui books designed for the person who wants to do a fuss-free Feng Shui.

More Titles under Joey Yap Books

Walking the Dragons

Compiled in one book for the first time from Joey Yap's Feng Shui Mastery Excursion Series, the book highlights China's extensive, vibrant history with astute observations on the Feng Shui of important sites and places. Learn the landform formations of Yin Houses (tombs and burial places), as well as mountains, temples, castles and villages.

Walking the Dragons : Taiwan Excursion

A Guide to Classical Landform Feng Shui of Taiwan

From China to Tibet, Joey Yap turns his analytical eye towards Taiwan in this extensive Walking the Dragons series. Combined with beautiful images and detailed information about an island once known as Formosa, or "Beautiful Island" in Portuguese, this compelling series of essays highlights the colourful history and wonders of Taiwan. It also provides readers with fascinating insights into the living science of Feng Shui.

The Art of Date Selection: Personal Date Selection (Available in English & Chinese)

With the Art of Date Selection: Personal Date Selection, you can learn simple, practical methods to select not just good dates, but personalised good dates as well. Whether it is a personal activity such as a marriage or professional endeavour, such as launching a business - signing a contract or even acquiring assets, this book will show you how to pick the good dates and tailor them to suit the activity in question, and to avoid the negative ones too!

Your Head Here

Your Head Here is the first book by Sherwin Ng. She is an accomplished student of Joey Yap, and an experienced Feng Shui consultant and instructor with Joey Yap Consulting Group and Mastery Academy respectively. It is the second book under the Fengshuilogy series, which focuses on Bedroom Feng Shui, a specific topic dedicated to optimum bed location and placement.

If the Shoe Fits

This book is for those who want to make the effort to enhance their relationship.

In her debut release, Jessie Lee humbly shares with you the classical BaZi method of the Ten Day Masters and the combination of a new profiling system developed by Joey Yap, to understand and deal with the people around you.

Being Happy and Successful at Work and in your Career

Have you ever wondered why some of us are so successful in our careers while others are dragging their feet to work or switching from one job to another? Janet Yung hopes to answer this question by helping others through the knowledge and application of BaZi and Chinese Astrology. In her debut release, she shares with the readers the right way of using BaZi to understand themselves: their inborn talents, motivations, skills, and passions, to find their own place in the path of professional development.

Being Happy & Successful - Managing Yourself & Others

Manage Your Talent & Have Effective Relationships at the Workplace

While many strive for efficiency in the workplace, it is vital to know how to utilize your talents. In this book, Janet Yung will take you further on how to use the BaZi profiling system as a tool to assess your personality and understanding your approach to the job. From ways in communicating with your colleagues to understanding your boss, you will be astounded by what this ancient system can reveal about you and the people in your life. Tips and guidance will also be given in this book so that you will make better decisions for your next step in advancing in your career.

Face Reading Collection

The Chinese Art of Face Reading: The Book of Moles

The Book of Moles by Joey Yap delves into the inner meanings of moles and what they reveal about the personality and destiny of an individual. Complemented by fascinating illustrations and Joey Yap's easy-to-understand commentaries and guides, this book takes a deeper focus into a Face Reading subject, which can be used for everyday decisions – from personal relationships to professional dealings and many others.

Discover Face Reading (Available in English & Chinese)

This is a comprehensive book on all areas of Face Reading, covering some of the most important facial features, including the forehead, mouth, ears and even philtrum above your lips. This book will help you analyse not just your Destiny but also help you achieve your full potential and achieve life fulfillment.

Joey Yap's Art of Face Reading

The Art of Face Reading is Joey Yap's second effort with CICO Books, and it takes a lighter, more practical approach to Face Reading. This book does not focus on the individual features as it does on reading the entire face. It is about identifying common personality types and characters.

Faces of Fortune: The 20 Tycoons to bet on over the next 10 years

Faces of Fortune is Tee Lin Say's first book on the subject of Mian Xiang or Chinese Face Reading. As an accomplished Face Reading student of Joey Yap and an experienced business journalist, Lin Say merged both her knowledge into this volume, profiling twenty prominent tycoons in Asia based on the Art of Face Reading.

Easy Guide on Face Reading (Available in English & Chinese)

The Face Reading Essentials series of books comprises of five individual books on the key features of the face – the Eyes, the Eyebrows, the Ears, the Nose, and the Mouth. Each book provides a detailed illustration and a simple yet descriptive explanation on the individual types of the features.

The books are equally useful and effective for beginners, enthusiasts and those who are curious. The series is designed to enable people who are new to Face Reading to make the most out of first impressions and learn to apply Face Reading skills to understand the personality and character of their friends, family, co-workers and business associates.

2017 Annual Releases

   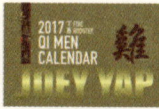   

| Chinese Astrology for 2017 | Feng Shui for 2017 | Tong Shu Desktop Calendar 2017 | Qi Men Desktop Calendar 2017 | Professional Tong Shu Diary 2017 | Tong Shu Monthly Planner 2017 | Weekly Tong Shu Diary 2017 |

www.masteryacademy.com | +6(03) - 2284 8080

Educational Tools and Software

Joey Yap's Feng Shui Template Set

Directions are the cornerstone of any successful Feng Shui audit or application. The Joey Yap Feng Shui Template Set is a set of three templates to simplify the process of taking directions and determining locations and positions, whether it is for a building, a house, or an open area such as a plot of land - all of it done with just a floor plan or area map.

The Set comprises three basic templates: The Basic Feng Shui Template, Eight Mansions Feng Shui Template, and the Flying Stars Feng Shui Template.

Mini Feng Shui Compass

The Mini Feng Shui Compass is a self-aligning compass that is not only light at 100gms but also built sturdily to ensure it will be convenient to use anywhere. The rings on the Mini Feng Shui Compass are bilingual and incorporate the 24 Mountain Rings that is used in your traditional Luo Pan.

The comprehensive booklet included with this, will guide you in applying the 24 Mountain Directions on your Mini Feng Shui Compass effectively and the Eight Mansions Feng Shui to locate the most auspicious locations within your home, office and surroundings. You can also use the Mini Feng Shui Compass when measuring the direction of your property for the purpose of applying Flying Stars Feng Shui.

MASTERY ACADEMY
OF CHINESE METAPHYSICS
Your **Preferred** Choice to the Art & Science of Classical Chinese Metaphysics Studies

Bringing **innovative** techniques and **creative** teaching methods to an ancient study.

Mastery Academy of Chinese Metaphysics was established by Joey Yap to play the role of disseminating this Eastern knowledge to the modern world with the belief that this valuable knowledge should be accessible to everyone and everywhere.

Its goal is to enrich people's lives through accurate, professional teaching and practice of Chinese Metaphysics knowledge globally. It is the first academic institution of its kind in the world to adopt the tradition of Western institutions of higher learning - where students are encouraged to explore, question and challenge themselves, as well as to respect different fields and branches of studies. This is done together with the appreciation and respect of classical ideas and applications that have stood the test of time.

The Art and Science of Chinese Metaphysics – be it Feng Shui, BaZi (Astrology), Qi Men Dun Jia, Mian Xiang (Face Reading), ZeRi (Date Selection) or Yi Jing – is no longer a field shrouded with mystery and superstition. In light of new technology, fresher interpretations and innovative methods, as well as modern teaching tools like the Internet, interactive learning, e-learning and distance learning, anyone from virtually any corner of the globe, who is keen to master these disciplines can do so with ease and confidence under the guidance and support of the Academy.

It has indeed proven to be a centre of educational excellence for thousands of students from over thirty countries across the world; many of whom have moved on to practice classical Chinese Metaphysics professionally in their home countries.

At the Academy, we believe in enriching people's lives by empowering their destinies through the disciplines of Chinese Metaphysics. Learning is not an option - it is a way of life!

MALAYSIA
19-3, The Boulevard, Mid Valley City, 59200 Kuala Lumpur, Malaysia
Tel : +6(03)-2284 8080 | Fax : +6(03)-2284 1218
Email : info@masteryacademy.com
Website : www.masteryacademy.com

Australia, Austria, Canada, China, Croatia, Cyprus, Czech Republic, Denmark, France, Germany, Greece, Hungary, India, Italy, Kazakhstan, Malaysia, Netherlands (Holland), New Zealand, Philippines, Poland, Russian Federation, Singapore, Slovenia, South Africa, Switzerland, Turkey, United States of America, Ukraine, United Kingdom

The Mastery Academy around the world!

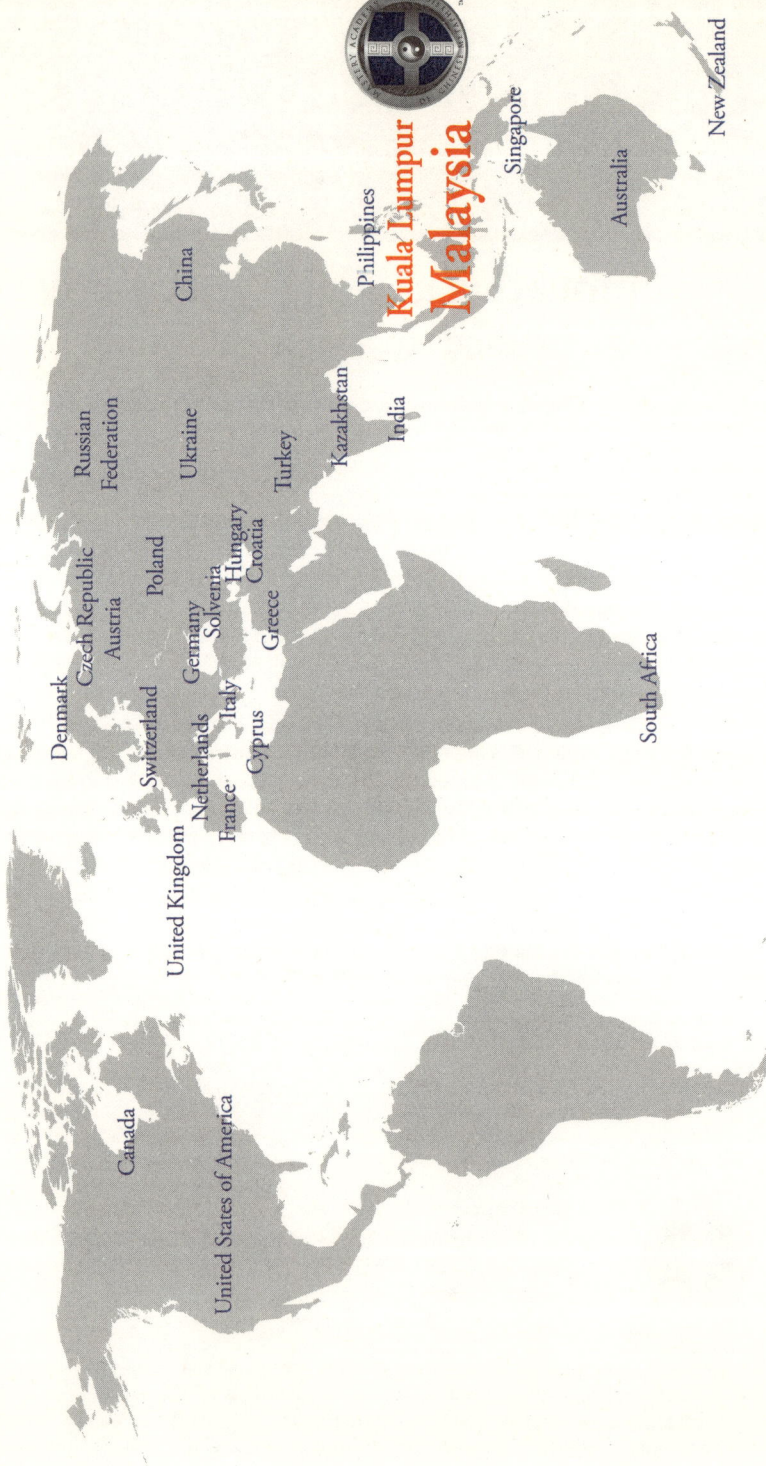

www.masteryacademy.com | +6(03) - 2284 8080

Feng Shui Mastery™
LIVE COURSES (MODULES ONE TO FOUR)

This an ideal program for those who wants to achieve mastery in Feng Shui from the comfort of their homes. This comprehensive program covers the foundation up to the advanced practitioner levels, touching upon the important theories from various classical Feng Shui systems including Ba Zhai, San Yuan, San He and Xuan Kong.

Module One: Beginners Course   **Module Two:** Practitioners Course   **Module Three:** Advanced Practitioners Course   **Module Four:** Master Course

BaZi Mastery™
LIVE COURSES (MODULES ONE TO FOUR)

This lesson-based program brings a thorough introduction to BaZi and guides the student step-by-step, all the way to the professional practitioner level. From the theories to the practical, BaZi students along with serious Feng Shui practitioners, can master its application with accuracy and confidence.

Module One: Intensive Foundation Course   **Module Two:** Practitioners Course   **Module Three:** Advanced Practitioners Course   **Module Four:** Master Course in BaZi

Xuan Kong Mastery™
LIVE COURSES (MODULES ONE TO THREE)
Advanced Courses For Master Practitioners

Xuan Kong is a sophisticated branch of Feng Shui, replete with many techniques and formulae, which encompass numerology, symbology and the science of the Ba Gua, along with the mathematics of time. This program is ideal for practitioners looking to bring their practice to a more in-depth level.

Module One: Advanced Foundation Course   **Module Two A:** Advanced Xuan Kong Methodologies   **Module Two B:** Purple White   **Module Three:** Advanced Xuan Kong Da Gua

www.masteryacademy.com | +6(03) - 2284 8080

Mian Xiang Mastery™
LIVE COURSES (MODULES ONE AND TWO)

This program comprises of two modules, each carefully developed to allow students to familiarise with the fundamentals of Mian Xiang or Face Reading and the intricacies of its theories and principles. With lessons guided by video lectures, presentations and notes, students are able to understand and practice Mian Xiang with greater depth.

Module One:
Basic Face Reading

Module Two:
Practical Face Reading

Yi Jing Mastery™
LIVE COURSES (MODULES ONE AND TWO)

Whether you are a casual or serious Yi Jing enthusiast, this lesson-based program contains two modules that brings students deeper into the Chinese science of divination. The lessons will guide students on the mastery of its sophisticated formulas and calculations to derive answers to questions we pose.

Module One:
Traditional Yi Jing

Module Two:
Plum Blossom Numerology

Ze Ri Mastery™
LIVE COURSES (MODULES ONE AND TWO)

In two modules, students will undergo a thorough instruction on the fundamentals of ZeRi or Date Selection. The comprehensive program covers Date Selection for both Personal and Feng Shui purposes to Xuan Kong Da Gua Date Selection.

Module One:
Personal and Feng Shui Date Selection

Module Two:
Xuan Kong Da Gua Date Selection

Joey Yap's
SAN YUAN QI MEN XUAN KONG DA GUA™

This is an advanced level program which can be summed up as the Integral Vision of San Yuan studies – an integration of the ancient potent discipline of Qi Men Dun Jia and the highly popular Xuan Kong 64 Hexagrams. Often regarded as two independent systems, San Yuan Qi Men and San Yuan Xuan Kong Da Gua can trace their origins to the same source and were actually used together in ancient times by great Chinese sages.

This method enables practitioners to harness the Qi of time and space, and predict the outcomes through a highly-detailed analysis of landforms, places and sites.

www.masteryacademy.com | +6(03) - 2284 8080

BaZi 10X

Emphasising on the practical aspects of BaZi, this programme is rich with numerous applications and techniques pertaining to the pursuit of wealth, health, relationship and career, all of which constitute the formula of success. This programme is designed for all levels of practitioners and is supplemented with innovative learning materials to enable easy learning. Discover the different layers of BaZi from a brand new perspective with BaZi 10X.

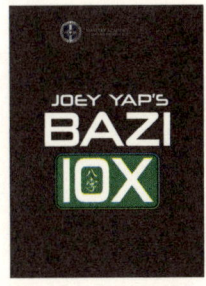

Feng Shui for Life

This is an entry-level five-day course designed for the Feng Shui beginner to learn the application of practical Feng Shui in day-to-day living. Lessons include quick tips on analysing the BaZi chart, simple Feng Shui solutions for the home, basic Date Selection, useful Face Reading techniques and practical Water formulas. A great introduction course on Chinese Metaphysics studies for beginners.

Joey Yap's Design Your Destiny

This is a three-day life transformation program designed to inspire awareness and action for you to create a better quality of life. It introduces the DRT™ (Decision Referential Technology) method, which utilises the BaZi Personality Profiling system to determine the right version of you, and serves as a tool to help you make better decisions and achieve a better life in the least resistant way possible, based on your Personality Profile Type.

Millionaire Feng Shui Secrets Programme

This program is geared towards maximising your financial goals and dreams through the use of Feng Shui. Focusing mainly on the execution of Wealth Feng Shui techniques such as Luo Shu sectors and more, it is perfect for boosting careers, businesses and investment opportunities.

Grow Rich With BaZi Programme

This comprehensive programme covers the foundation of BaZi studies and presents information from the career, wealth and business standpoint. This course is ideal for those who want to maximise their wealth potential and live the life they deserve. Knowledge gained in this course will be used as driving factors to encourage personal development towards a better future.

Walk the Mountains!
Learn Feng Shui in a Practical and Hands-on Program

 ### Feng Shui Mastery Excursion™

Learn landform (Luan Tou) Feng Shui by walking the mountains and chasing the Dragon's vein in China. This program takes the students in a study tour to examine notable Feng Shui landmarks, mountains, hills, valleys, ancient palaces, famous mansions, houses and tombs in China. The excursion is a practical hands-on course where students are shown to perform readings using the formulas they have learnt and to recognise and read Feng Shui Landform (Luan Tou) formations.

Read about the China Excursion here:
http://www.fengshuiexcursion.com

Mastery Academy courses are conducted around the world. Find out when will Joey Yap be in your area by visiting
www.masteryacademy.com
or call our offices at **+6(03)-2284 8080**.

Online Home Study Courses

Gain Valuable Knowledge from the Comfort of Your Home

Now, armed with your trusty computer or laptop and Internet access, the knowledge of Chinese Metaphysics is just a click away!

3 Easy Steps to Activate Your Home Study Course:

Step 1:
Go to the URL as indicated on the Activation Card and key in your Activation Code

Step 2:
At the Registration page, fill in the details accordingly to enable us to generate your Student Identification (Student ID).

Step 3:
Upon successful registration, you may begin your lessons immediately.

Joey Yap's Feng Shui Mastery HomeStudy Course

Module 1: **Empowering Your Home**
Module 2: **Master Practitioner Program**

Learn how easy it is to harness the power of the environment to promote health, wealth and prosperity in your life. The knowledge and applications of Feng Shui will not be a mystery but a valuable tool you can master on your own.

Joey Yap's BaZi Mastery HomeStudy Course

Module 1: **Mapping Your Life**
Module 2: **Mastering Your Future**

Discover your path of least resistance to success with insights about your personality and capabilities, and what strengths you can tap on to maximise your potential for success and happiness by mastering BaZi (Chinese Astrology). This course will teach you all the essentials you need to interpret a BaZi chart and more.

Joey Yap's Mian Xiang Mastery HomeStudy Course

Module 1: **Face Reading**
Module 2: **Advanced Face Reading**

A face can reveal so much about a person. Now, you can learn the Art and Science of Mian Xiang (Chinese Face Reading) to understand a person's character based on his or her facial features, with ease and confidence.

www.masteryacademy.com | +6(03) - 2284 8080